ONLY LOVE IS POURING

B Prior

First Published in 2019

BERNIE PRIOR FOUNDATION LTD

30 Teddington Rd, Governors Bay,
RD1 Lyttelton, New Zealand

Contents

Prologue   **5**
Tuscany Retreat   **9**
  Opening Night   11
  Day One   17
  Day Two   33
  Day Three   41
  Day Four   49
  Day Five   61
Crete Retreat   **67**
  Day One   69
  Day Two   75
  Day Three   79
  Day Four   83
  Day Five   85
  Day Six   87
  Day Seven   91
  Day Eight   93
  Day Nine   97
  Day Ten   99
  Day Eleven   107
  Day Twelve   111
New Zealand Retreat   **123**
  Opening Night   125
  Day One   131
  Day Two   137
  Day Three   141
  Day Four   145
  Day Five   151
About B   **156**

Prologue

This book is a day by day compilation of quotes, short pieces, pointers and awakening gems that stem from three residential retreats with visionary teacher B Prior during the year 2017.

Unimaginable journeys into the depth of Being and beyond, they are a manifestation of life's highest and most precious calling to return to Source and be the vibrant expression of All that one *already* is.

Every retreat is unique in its flow and unfoldment; moment by moment, day by day, listener and speaker merge in a growing field of depth, original power and communion.

B's words and transmission ignite a light, spark a remembrance within. He brings universal truth into the very cells of one's body, where it begins to live in every breath.

Themes emerge, like countless threads, weaving a fabric that is as much a unique expression of the colours, shapes and experiences that define the human condition as it is the very translucency through which the ineffable shines; preceding yet permeating all things.

The sessions are unscripted, conversational, always *New-Now*, touching all aspects of life: relationships, sexuality, death and dying, children, work and creativity laying it *all* into the heart of knowing Awareness.

The writing is kept in line with B's verbal style to fully
maintain the essence and transmission of his teaching.

Be slow and silent in your reading, allow the words to
drop into a space of open receptivity and they will
reveal the fragrance of that which is forever beyond
expression.

Tuscany Retreat

"It is the unfamiliar that is your love, not the familiar.
The unfamiliar brings you alive and awake.
That is where you are really safe,
where you are uncontained.
The familiar is not safe, it passes away.
The unfamiliar does not pass away.
Those that live in an unfamiliar subtle way of Being
will not pass away."

Opening Night

*"Let's spend the entire retreat recognising the door,
which is our heart, to the deep."*

Hear My Call From Within

We may never leave this place alive!
We will definitely leave this place changed and not only
this place will change but *we* will change, simply by
way of remembering who we are.

Nothing is planned, nothing is written down,
nothing is thought about. All this will just unfold. It is
the truth of what we are as Pure Awareness.

Where I come from, all phenomenal form arises in what
I already Am and all phenomenal form resolves in
'What I Am'. I have no need to touch it. If I touch it as
a believed 'someone' I add time to the form, whereas all
forms really are in timeless Awareness and all form
truly is pure form Now.

I don't ask you to believe or understand any of what I
say, I just ask you to come and enjoy Being together. I
will call you and you will hear me call from within. You
might look twice: "Did he call me there? How is he in
here? Is he 'there' or here, or is the one who is speaking,
the one who is listening, the one who is hearing the
same One?"

Love Pouring - The Eyes of a Newborn

What we are about to look at is the basis and ground of the entire life of the living universe. Certainly this will be the ground of everything we could ever possibly share together on this retreat. Very simple… We are going to return to being babies!

Is there anyone who has never seen a newborn? Ok, everyone has seen a newly born child. We look at a newborn and our mind, our conditioning tells us: 'That's a child', but when you look into the eyes of a child, do you actually see a child or do you see the deep? And as you look into the deep, it is pure 'Nothing–Aware', pure emptiness or Pure Being.

The mind is convinced that that is a baby, but what you love as you look into a newborn's eyes, is that you are knowing where you come from. You are looking into your own unborn state and It is looking back at you. This is Love pouring.

Although we believe our conditioning when we look at a baby, if we go just a little bit deeper we discover something other than a child, it is a being. But are you looking into one being or are you looking into a whole realm of Pure Awareness, looking back, a realm of Pure Awareness with countless nameless beings pouring out? You *are* that, you *are* the outpouring.

You look into the child's eyes and the light you see is light pouring out of deep, black, pure, endless, Awareness. It is so thrilling, not because it is a baby, but because it's 'You', Pure You. You can call it Pure Awareness or God.

What enthrals you so is that you remember and apprehend *What You Are* and how you came into this form. But did you? Did you come into this form or are you unborn? Not a form, unformed and although you are pouring out into existence, phenomenal form is what is dancing in your own Pure Awareness.

There is a whole realm of deep Beingness pouring out. It might look like 'one being' but that one being is made up by a whole movement of a deeper formless realm.

Humans may not realise this but the entire conditional realm is influencing each apparent individual. Therefore, how can we say that our thoughts, our feelings and even our sensations are our own? What I am pointing to is: only the deep is moving, only the deep is knowing, only the deep is seeing and only the deep is becoming. This is Love's outpouring.

A baby knows no form, knows no other, knows no 'thing'. A baby has no experience. If it could speak it could only say: "I Am. I am Pure Awareness knowing I am aware."

The baby you see is not what the baby knows. It's a being. It doesn't know form, doesn't differentiate Consciousness and its forms. It doesn't know it has 'a hand' that it moves. The baby moves but it has no hand. It is told that it has a hand later.

If you close your eyes and just move your hand, is there really a hand moving or is it Being moving? What is first the Being or the form? Isn't it Being moving and as Being moves it forms? Being moves, form appears. A child doesn't touch 'a table', it is moving in its own true formlessness.

Why it goes:"Aaaahhh!" and smiles is because on the existent realm it forms, its movement on this realm is forming! If the baby could speak it would go: "My God! How did I do that?!" It has no relationship with formal form. Its total joy is the magic of the movement of its being, the utter enjoyment of what it already is, non-dual; no subject, no object, just the pouring of its own being, which is Love.

The innocence of the child is Beingness - so pure! Later it discovers that its movement is forming and investigates this forming. First it doesn't find any separation, it is taught that. It is taught separation. The first form of separation, the first duality is the child's name.

Let's call our child: 'Sonia'. "Sonia… Sonia? Sonia!!!!" If you look at this, your name is the constant programming that you are a 'someone'. But you are so enjoying being no one! The name is the first pattern of duality but there is a miracle spinning as well. Did you not know that you are spinning your forms of experience now?

Your name is the first duality but also the first highest possibility to individuate but not separate. Nothing-Aware. That's *What You Are*; no-thing, 'Nothing-

Aware.' The name is a singular possibility of 'Nothing-Aware', a point in which Awareness can become creative.

The baby is not a someone, it is not a something. It is pure No-thing-Awareness, there are many names for that: The Self, Pure Awareness, God, Love.

The movement of that child is the movement of Pure Being with no beginning and end. You have, we have, no beginning and end.

That first outpouring is a dimension within the Self, outpouring into an apparent human life. When a parent is teaching a child to take the first step for instance, they may believe that it is about a physical step, about 'how to walk as a human being', but to the beingness of the child that is not a step, let's say in the living room. It is its first step as Beingness into the entire human psyche and even bigger than that. It is the first universal step of a being into the universe. That's how big it is.

I am only speaking of Love and goodness and the purpose behind all this is for Self to realise Self, Love to realise Love and Awareness to be All that it can be aware in.

Day One

"Walk amongst any dualities being non-dual, singularly inspired by The Self. Feel it. It is Here Now. Then you walk amongst the world and are not of it."

Nothing-Aware Remains

Are you sure that you are aware? Is it not true that 'Nothing-Aware' remains? No matter how your person moves, how a sense of self functions, wherever, whoever? Nothing-Aware remains the ground of all experience. Look now, it's still deep. It's not dependent on a sense of self or person. It's not dependent on the weather, not dependent on human bodies or bodies of the universe. All may pass away but Nothing-Aware remains. When you become opened, *all* is silent goodness.

Look at our analogy of the baby: its silence is unborn. Even its love is unborn although it can move up and express in existence. And as unborn silence moves, the cosmos is immediately formed and moving. That's why sometimes in our experience of waking up in the morning or going to sleep at night, the sounds of nature or others are nothing but fading silhouettes, friends we say goodbye to, as we move home.

Silent Roots in Your Inner Garden

Notice how your inner garden is already changing. Silent roots of deeper dimensions are opening. These are pointers. Your ability as Awareness to see and know these silent roots growing is your growing ability to respond to pure Knowing on the level of humanness. When awakened Awareness opening in a human body has gone through some self-emptying, it begins to match the finer garden within. Awareness responding to Knowing then moves a different life. When Awareness responding to Knowing moves, deeper realms open within and opportunities arrive without. This is Non - Duality. The unseen and the seen is made of the same stuff, known by the Only One.

In a very practical way the surface life is moved by the deeper Knowing. Opportunities that appear to come from this world or from form, are actually the movement of 'beyond'. This world does not make itself. That is an illusion. This world is made of Pure Consciousness; conditional, but its ground is pure. A movement of any world is Nothing-Aware moving by Knowing. Not by thoughts, not by feelings. Thoughts and feelings are the interpretation of experience. When deeper levels move up to the surface, in and as Awareness having human form, this deeper movement opens the perception and there is pure sensation within a vast space of nothingness. Goodness fills the heart, filling up the body-mind. No interpretation. Nothing-Aware fulfilled by Knowing. The Self that came out of the absolute Awareness is what Awareness is looking for; Itself.

One Drop of Your Essence

Somewhere you are mixed up as to what life is. Life is not this little life of sense objects and this subject called 'me'. That's a puddle. Life is an ocean! When we drop into deep dreamless sleep, that is Life. Look at your life, the concepts you hold about 'Who I Am'.

Look to see how you move in 'like and dislike' and not pure Knowing. Let go of these dualities. Not easy, because this world is an enormous pressure of likes and dislikes. But if you take just one drop of your essence and drop it into the world, the whole world will change. That's how vast *What You Are* is. *This* is satsang.

Awakening to a Deeper Functionality

B speaks about a movie about Jesus:

At the end of the film, Jesus says to the disciples: "I have now prepared the place for you to come. Find me within you."

This is satsang! If a being really has realised The Self, then the way is being made. No one's doing it. It's just the truth of *the* Self realising itself. Satsang is you being Nothing-Aware, moving by Knowing. Responding to Knowing, not listening to the noise of the self, the person or the world. That's your movement. Clearly you know you are not the body-mind, then why function as if you are one. Awaken to deeper functionality. The deeper realms of your own brightness have a function but it is entirely different than sense perception. This is

why you can't get there from here. You discover, I have
always been *Here* never there! I *am* the way. I *am* the
door. I *am* this One.

This what you begin to remember as formed ideas shed
from your psyche and structures of egoity fall away
from your perception.

Move the deeper Knowing. Your sense of self and
person will also move and you will be experiencing the
patterning of that level coming home. Amongst the
changes that take place you remain Nothing-Aware
responding to Knowing moving. You are so open, that
as Awareness you can read the levels of self, *your* self
and the deeper invitations of realising that are taking
place in the inner. You are the One that is moving
through those levels. Moving as Nothing-Aware
Knowing through those levels is Oneness moving. You
are uniting those innermost levels, all the way out.

Have you ever seen a river from high up in an airplane?
You see the river and many other streams joining the
river. That's Oneness moving. The river moving through
all the levels of the land and each stream is being made
into one movement within the river. In the same way all
your levels are united by your movement to being
Truth. It doesn't have to feel good, it *is* the Good
moving.

The Answer is Already What I Am

The earth can't answer itself. Humanness can't answer
itself. The world cannot answer itself. It keeps itself the
same by answering itself. Within satsang we discover
the answer is 'What I Am' already. As we are sharing
together, watch how Awareness still seeks answers
through familiarity, through the familiar sense of self,
person and other. There are no answers there. These are
all dualities. They are themselves instruments arising in
Awareness. They have no power of their own. Return to
your heart, the heart that doesn't belong to the sense of
person, self or other. The heart is where Awareness
unmistakably realises its Self that is streaming.

Un-awakened Awareness appearing in human form,
mainly struggles with the circumstances and difficulties
of life. It has not yet realised that it is its own answer.
Awareness knowing it knows is the answer: Self-
realisation.

Clearly, what is being spoken here will be filtered
through the dualities of this realm, but I speak to you
direct, no filter. A way of Being that is instant, pure,
immediate. When Nothing-Aware returns to Knowing
in human form, when Nothing-Aware discovers its pure
Knowing at the level of the heart, it opens the door to
Self-realisation and revelation.

Without Awareness relating to the heart in human form,
the deeper unseen levels have no way into human form.
You must return to being the heart. Then as the heart it
answers life; outpouring and returning are the same
movement. Although that opening seems to take time, it

is immediate on the level of the heart and deeper. But as
that Knowing enters the stream of body-mind
experience, the information given on the human level
will be very much the same. Walk amongst those
dualities being non-dual. Singularly inspired by The
Self. Feel it. It is Here Now. Then you walk amongst
the world and are not of it. You certainly don't judge it.
Compassion takes place for the difficulties of those that
are awakening in this realm. But then you laugh and
you may cry and you laugh because this is all a game;
there *is* only God everywhere.

Difficult to hear right? Especially when there is
suffering or pain. When the body drops away you will
know this. How deeply you will be able to move in the
Knowing, in many ways is determined by how you open
in the beyond whilst having form. Form gives you
instant reflection of what you are being and how you are
moving. Whatever frequency that is always forms.

We are returning to our heart and becoming stabilised in
the heart and deeper. There are no answers to this
conditionality *from* this conditionality. The one who is
listening to these words now *is* the answer. As you
realise this and respond to this, you will shed all the
shields you have placed over your heart and experience.

You stop. You look and see into the Knowing and the
Knowing welcomes you home, the Knowing answers
the forming of moving life and love. Your person, your
self evolves and you awaken to the deep and are able to
move as the deep in the person and the self. The body is
remade and re-encoded from this awakening.

This is my way. I am not one who says: "Oneness that's it. All is God, get on with it." No, the realisation here is, the one who is listening is the Absolute. There is nothing but God or the Self in varied experiences of Consciousness. The Self is, by doing nothing, evolving everything. The one who is listening, including the speaker, is That.

I teach transcendence and manifesting that. There is Nothing-Aware responding to Knowing. There is no 'doing' in that, no 'someone' in that. Awareness-Knowing moving creates the cosmos. The Self is awakening to Itself on a level of reality and it is 'I'.

A Disturbing Force of Love

On the level of the experience of the body-mind integration that takes place as Awareness stays true to Knowing in human form. One man said: "Your mother will hate you, your father will hate you, your brothers and sisters will hate you if you come unto me."

This simply means, Awareness awakening to itself in the realm of conditionality, displaces this conditional realm. People no longer recognise each other but they begin to recognise what they are at Source. All your relationships are being displaced by you awakening as Awareness. Nobody can relate in the usual way. There is no basis to continue the same old way of relating, through you awakening. You are a disturbing force of Love!

As you awaken to your awakening in the heart, you *are* the way. *You* are the way. Walk amongst all this undoing, naked, open and receiving. Meeting Being to Being, heart to heart, despite the fire and the burning. Then what you will do is the burning of the patterning. It will be the fuel of your awakening and the awakening of those available to realise in your company. *You* be the meeting place, fully accept you are returning to the Source as your Self. Then you invite in each meeting, Being to Being, the undoing of patterning of separation. That energy returns to your heart and you welcome it home. As the pattern returns and you are open it moves into a new form of deeper Knowing. It's transformed into transcendental presence and Awareness, for the table is made of God, the murderer is made of God, pain is made of God, ALL is made of God.

All is Welcome!

All is welcome in this house of Love. Discover what that really means. You are without beginning and end. Take the opportunity in this life to discover the love of That that you truly are. Familiarity? Well, you begin to have clarity about your familiarity! A situation might come where your lover is screaming at you or your friend or your family and you go: "Good friend, I see you again. Welcome, you and I have been friends since the beginning of time!" Rumi and Hafiz have poems about this.

It seems to be that someone over there is doing this but it is the pattern of the universe longing to meet its God or its Good. You are meeting it. It's not someone doing

something to you but it is the patterns of the universe
longing to meet its source. Welcome it, now fully open,
"Welcome, you are not my enemy. You are my long
lost love! Welcome. You did not betray me, I betrayed
me by not knowing who I am. Welcome."

Deep real inner resolution of the divine, meeting
humanness. You never did anything, you never caused
anything. You were never separate. You were always
whole. Never were you anything else but The Self.
Awareness surrenders to the sweetness of knowing it
knows. Old levels dissolve. Awareness is unobscured
from its own Love-light.

Everything Moves Because of You

Everything in the universe, everything that grows,
everything that moves, is moving because of You.
When I say 'you' I mean you as Awareness. Nothing-
Aware, knowingly aware of form in its own Awareness.
The truth that you are knowingly aware calls the deep to
know you and you to know the deep. That meeting
moves the universe by the very truth that *What You Are*
in the deepest place is Nothing-Aware knowing
Knowing.

You know you are aware. Maybe you are coming upon
'you are No-thing aware' and knowing you are not an
object and maybe even knowing you are Knowing;
aware Consciousness itself.

All phenomenal form is arising in Awareness-Knowing.
Your body, the universe, all things. You are awakening

in the phenomenal form in your own knowing
Awareness.

The moment you move to understand this by the use of
thought feeling or sense of self, you fall into
identification with the forms. The moment You,
'Nothing-Aware Knowing', cease using a familiar sense
of self to know, knowing comes easily.

You begin to realise you are not using a sense of self to
know you know. Have you ever experienced deep
dreamless sleep? We all have. That's because you are
aware Knowing. It is the continuum of your experience.
It knows no beginning and no end. You are 'there' in
deep dreamless sleep. You didn't need objects or a sense
of self to tell you anything.

Maybe you have a touch of understanding of this and
then it will seem to evaporate. This is because you are
not moving at the absolute speed of knowing Knowing
as yet. You relate to experience through a subject and
an object, but in deep dreamless sleep there is no
objective experience. You really are the Absolute, but
you seem to think that you cannot move at the absolute
speed of Knowing. But you are already knowing the
Knowing of the deep. That's why you sit in satsang and
you have a calling to speak of Truth, Love or Life. You
are Knowing knowing the deep.

Take Yourself Off The Cross

Q: *My question is about this sense of a threat that I am experiencing about fully being What I Am.*

I had this sensation today of being right there on the cross. I was on the cross like Christ and saying: "Yes, I am scared and it is ok that I am scared in this situation."

B: I would ask you to ask the question: Who is scared? Who is it? Is that just another phenomenal experience? Is that more phenomenal movement? How deep do you want to go?

I am suggesting to *What You Are*: move from the knowing of your being, giving up making stories of a sense of self, giving up translating sensation into feelings and thoughts.

You will never know fear. This is what awakening is about, to dissolve all the distractions of the body-mind identification. Stepping back, stepping deep, stepping back, stepping deep through the porthole of the heart. Seeing and knowing and moving as Awareness.

You know, I was nine years old, I was home alone and it was very dark. I was on my own in the living room and I remember experiencing a very unknown strange movement. It came from inside. It wasn't outside and the light coming through the window refracted. In that moment lightning and thunder happened. Suddenly there was fear in the body, but not in me, and Jesus walked through the window. Walked through the

window and spoke without his lips moving and I fell
with Him into a deep love. All fear evaporated and I
only knew this being, being me.

This happened similarly when I was four. Four! I was
having my tonsils removed and I remember my eldest
sister came to see me in hospital. She brought me a tiny
little book, which for me was big, and in it there were
pictures of Jesus speaking to children and he moved and
spoke to me on the page. He just said: "Go! Go to What
This Is." I woke up after the operation and the presence
of the being stayed in my heart. I had many other beings
coming to me as child.

He was never on the cross. In the truest sense. He
brought true relationship to the vertical and the
horizontal. That cross is not a burden. It is magical
mystical love. Life is not a burden. It is the wildest
opportunity to realise you are God.

More than anything I am suggesting, never listen to
hand-me-down information. You don't know whether he
died or not and if he was on the cross. Did he survive it?
Did his body transfigure or was his DNA ignited by the
depth of his mystery? Did his whole body return into
the mystery intact? Is this not the destiny you know of
this planet called humanness?

Behold your Self. Discover *You*. Dive into the deep and
let that answer the moment of life. Don't listen to
anything that ever existed, ever. No past, no future, no
history, no other. Only listen to the deep in you.

You'll still be able to walk in the world: polar experiences of a separate sense of self, appearing in space and time. The brain doing its mystical job of dividing one whole reality into many parts of expression, the individuation of Consciousness and its movement of form.

Rather than listen to the conditionality, dive through the door of your heart for your being is deeper than your heart and respond to the deep Knowing knowing.

You might be afraid that you'll be outcast from your friends and your family and culture. But all that conditioning passes away. You do not. Be true to the deeper Knowing. Cease moving as if you belong to space and time. Space and time make it possible to have three-dimensional form to express the uniqueness of one sense of self.

You don't know whether he died. But if you want to put yourself on a cross, then there are plenty of nails around. One is: (*B speaks like a robot*) "I don't like this. I don't like that. This should be different. That should be different. How is this possible?" How many more nails do you want? You are abandoning this idea that you're a separate-sensed self. Recognise, when you wake in the morning, the body becomes illumed. You're the one that makes all this possible and all the information in the body-mind is information since time seems to have begun. *What You Are* is big enough to be in this but not of it. That is self-mastery and real love.

Take yourself off the cross!

Do you need some hands? It is fine to have Love-hands.

Q: *I really got the answer and this urgency was there because in these last months I really created some very real physical threats and I couldn't handle it anymore.*

B: This is something you can really understand and the understanding could be instant. What Y ou Are as 'non-physical' becomes instantly physical. Everything becomes physical for What you Are, whilst you have a human body-form.

The deepest level of realisation, the Self, will become physical for you. Self-transformation and realisation, physically taking place. That's the purpose of form, to make the deep physical, formed. The embodiment of That that needs no body. It is a miracle: "Wow!"

When your body drops away, you will see a light and you will recognise where I am speaking from. You'll go: "That's the door B pointed me to! "I will be there waiting. Come to this dimension of life! You will see many beings are heading to the lights that they were realising. They don't recognise each other. They only recognise the ones that were moving in the same door. A realised being realises all beings, all doors, all places lead to the One. That is your destiny right now, whilst you have a body. I am encouraging you to go all the way in.

Reach into the unknown. All the hands of familiarity will be pulling you back. You just kiss those hands. You leave them alone and continue moving into the deep. When you die, the place from which you have been functioning will welcome you home. You are not human; this humanity is just one level of forming.

Cease performing, let go of acting and be your Self. Ignore everything else. That doesn't mean you shut everything down. It means knowing clearly, 'I am going home.' Utterly open, you reach into the deep because you are moving there Now. The level you are moving into then moves into this level of forming. That higher level grows this level.

This is still quite rare on this earth. We have become so distracted from what we are and we want tangible evidence. Well, here it is: deep dreamless sleep. You know you slept well, no form, no self, no other but you know.

Day Two

"Wherever you are,
deeper streams of your love,
deeper streams of your being, a
greater depth of What You Are
is the one constant that is present."

What is First?

The one who is reading the moment, the one that is reading the book, reading the flower, the face, the friendship, the hate and the despair, that one is Love. And it is only ever reading its own Love, which in existence appears so differently to what it actually is.

What is first when you close your eyes and gently lift your palms up?

What is in this black?

Are you knowing your hands or are you knowing deeper Knowing?

And as you move your hands, is that a movement of your hands or is that a movement of knowing Knowing?

Does form follow your movement of Knowing or is Knowing following forms of experience?

See what is first. Is the form of experience of body-mind first and 'What I Am' last?

Am I putting what is last, first and what is first, last?

The world you are in is upside down, the wrong way up.
It puts form first and the *knowing* of form last. Turn
inside out. Knowing Knowing is the first; it is the first,
the middle and the end.

You are not looking into the black, you *are* the
Absolute; no-thing and how you know this is the light
of Knowing that pours from your absolute-ness. *You* are
pouring this moment, from the profound all the way to
the surface. All is profound in your profundity of
presence.

Form follows the law of Love, it forms what you
Awareness, are belonging to.

The Gold of Soul to Soul

Oh such packaging! You packaged all those patterns
very well! Some have red ribbons on, red-ribboned
patterns, some are packaged with duct tape, some are
quite greasy. It's funny how you put this stuff together.

Don't worry, none of it safe with me! It's not safe with
me. It will definitely return to Nothing and I will give it
back to you, changed.

That's what we are doing, we are giving each other our
selves, changed. We don't look into each other's eyes to
keep ourselves the same. We look into each other's eyes
to be changed. We don't want to change, we look to *be*
changed, to see and know as the One.

Be changed. Open. No need to have the pennies. You want gold. You want the gold of soul to soul, Being to Being, Love to Love. Now, if as Being to Being you want to share your burden on the level of self, this is the best place to do it. First we know One, not two, then we can be One-two, a movement of Knowing, moving in twoness which equals Oneness.

You have to recognise when there is a level of self and person you still want to keep. Why? Shine your light of Knowing on it...

The Unifying Centre

What You Are is the unifying centre of *all* experience. That's why it is so powerful, this illusory belief that you're a body-mind; because you have believed it so. Millions of patterns moving power and images, all held together in singularity, by *You*. It's very powerful, the power to separate that that is singular.

You're trying to trust your sense of self? There is only one thing you can trust there: your power to unify all the movements of illusion. That's really powerful, because you are the ground of all experience. 'I Am' is your very first experience. You can even say that in deep dreamless sleep. I Am aware. You know, 'I slept well', but really there was no object in your awareness. *You* are the ground.

Your Word

Listen to when you speak. What happens when you speak? Isn't each word the sound of the universe? Are you not knowing the Knowing as you speak?

On this level of forming, your word is your prior state, forming. It is a very fine vibrational thing, but words show you what you are forming.

You will use less words as you go finer within, but you won't know if your word is your word, is your bond until you speak it. Then you are able to know how meaningful you are in your word.

When you hear yourself speak you are also knowing how meaningfully and how true to your word you are moving. Are the vehicles of perception, person, heart and body aligned with what you are saying? How far is the river of meaning flowing? All the way out? How far is it flowing?

Yes, we do get to a place of 'no need to verbalise' but this can also be a wonderful escape route. You can use 'not speaking' as a little escape. Awareness can still protect its forms and not truly know the state of the forms it is moving.

When you speak, discover that your word shows you Awareness, whether you are moving as meaning. See, how the word is known in your body in your heart, in your system. Don't use your brain, use your body to know. Your word is your bond to you being meaning. You will know the sound of the forms that you relate to

that are not integrated in your being when you speak.
And when speak and you are moving as deeper
meaning, the forms in your life that are integrated in
your heart of Being will sound different.

We speak so that we really know what we 'have' as
Awareness and what we have as a separate sense of self.
It gives us an instant measure of the instant evolution of
our forms and our Awareness in existence.

If you don't speak, you can pretend those forms are all
aligned. This mystery needs conversation. It needs
engagement.
This is why I encourage you to speak. Listen to what
you say. Everything is a feedback. The entire universe
is feeding back the meaning of you and how *What You
Are* is evolving the universe of your forming.

I Am the word, I Am the movement of the word. I Am
the sound of the word. I Am the forms of that word. I
Am the way of the word *and* I Am beyond the word. I
Am the sound of the universe creating, dissolving and
returning to the 'I' that I Am.

Listen to what you say. Otherwise you will just be
ordinary and not get in touch with the extraordinary.
Awake, awake!

Your House

How is your house? Are you living in a meaningful place that vibes with your intention of true life? How many comfort stories are you stacking into your bricks? How many comfort stories are living in your armchairs? Do you walk into your house and it inspires your soul or does it inspire your small self? "Oh, thank God, I am home! Oh, this world is so...! Oh, those people! Oh, thank God for you sofa, you understand I need rest."

Go into your living room with your heart, be in your heart in your living room. Understand, this is the living room; LIVING room! From your heart, what are you truly seeing and knowing in your living room? It can take you to the heart of your soul or to the little bit of comfort that you believe you need.
Step into your living room as a heart. Does it match the deeper meaning of you? Then your living room is going to reveal the universe to you and your innermost until the whole universe is your living room.

One Destination

The entire cosmos and all beings in it, has one destination: Self-realisation; the One who is in it, moving it and beyond it. Everything that could possibly ever happen is engineered by that One.

That is awakening. That is *What You Are* as nothing, as Nothing-Aware. Your ability as Awareness to be in any level of Consciousness that you are presented with, is the evolution of all your forms and the evolution of you as Awareness.

You *are* Awareness and you *have* Knowing. Clearly, to have experience there must be Consciousness or life force and for you to be consciously aware within experience, fully awake in that experience, as Awareness itself leads you to Self-realisation.

In That Moment I Exist

Allow life to be your opportunity to completely open up. Then you discover that you are openness. Pure Awareness in which the Truth moves.

Imagine a completely black space, like when you close you eyes. Whilst you have a body-mind you think you are looking as a 'someone' into that black space, but you are the totality of the endless Nothing.

The light by which you know yourself comes out of the black, a tiny little mustard seed and it fills the perception. In that moment 'I exist'. The Self is expressing the endlessness of Awareness.

Day Three

*"You are the new testament to the truth
you move as the Self. You are the book of Life.
You are the transcendental One."*

We Pour Into the Universe

When a baby awakens in the morning, when that being
enters the realm of body-mind, it doesn't know it is
doing that. It discovers that later, because at that stage it
is not individuated Consciousness. It is All that is.

Let's imagine we are babies and we awake in the
morning. We fill up the universe instantly. We don't
open to a cot. We don't look for Mum and Dad. We
don't have a separate home and a separate body. We
pour into the universe as a totality, a singular movement
of the deep. No one is there. No one, just wholeness,
wonder, fullness.

The baby opens its eyes into the universe. It is not
individuated. The outpouring is instant. In one teaching
they call it the holy instant. There is no one here, only
that One.

When you awaken you are remembering how you fill
up the space. You are taking down the walls, the fences,
the doors, the burglar alarm. You are opening up. You
will be in the experience of opening up to what you
closed down to.

Dismantling Polarity

When you come upon a like or dislike, you can open the like or dislike deeper than its opposite. When you open a like or dislike, which is basically polarity, it dismantles as a polarity. You are dismantling the polarity of your separate sense of self. In dismantling likes and dislikes you re-enter your singularity, your heart. You begin to know and deepen in Being.

You are seeing and knowing as a being. Every sinew of the body is encoded with Beingness. The deeper levels of the body respond to the being of Truth.

The surface levels of the body are in change when you respond to being true. Your face changes, the nervous system changes, the heart opens, the body opens and life is fulfilling. The deeper purpose of existence begins to shine. Self-realisation and the movement of manifestation as its expression.

As you Awareness re-enter the heart through Being, all your sensory forms, psychic and energetic forms begin to move towards the 'I' and come through you for transformation. Within this transformation Awareness discovers deeper levels and realms of its being, which then begin to form.

In this you as a being are full of purpose and meaning. It's not as it was when you were a separate sense of self. It has no want or need in it. You have returned to when you were a child, where opened loveliness is moving. You begin to move the deep, landing it into form, through your heart.

Your body, which is truly a hologram, held together on the surface with divine intention, begins to download higher realms of Being and is a constant flow of the deep moving out into form. Form is in change to manifest the continuum of deep revelation. This level is designed to change. You, Awareness-Knowing are the one constant amongst this change.

This is the Self revealing itself, knowing itself, loving itself, forming itself, dissolving itself - all returning home. Constant expression, constant return - infinite. This life is radiant stillness.

Truth is Immediate

"Once I was blind but now I see"… now I see from a deeper level of me. You perceive deeper. Perception is always in existence. You could perceive a star system two hundred billion light years away and yet the *knowing* of the place that is light years away is the immediacy that *you are* it.

Light moves slowly, so slow! Truth is immediate: I *am* That.

You are awakening in quite a solid conditionality and this level of information tells you that it takes time to love, it takes time to realise, it takes time to do anything. But it takes no time to love, no time to realise but to form that will take time. It is a gathering of lights and information moving to form and the movement of that universal energy is held together by your belonging to the deep.

You have no idea that you are putting all of this together. All your likes and dislikes are in your own hands. You are holding your life in your own hands. You want to Self-realise or to realise Love, whilst you're holding onto polarities, likes and dislikes.

You will have to let it all go for the deeper level to form what that looks like. At the moment, to bring that it takes time to form, but it takes no time for you to walk in the shadows of your past and be in the presence of your realising Love now.

The shadows will just fade and new life begins to sprout. The old leaves fall to the ground and are good manure for the new flowering. The emptying out of this realm of the identity with past experience is taking place.

There *is* a space not too far beyond this world where Consciousness travels far faster and forms far faster, were it takes no time to form what you already are.

What happens in satsang is not ordinariness. The lights go to a place where you are available and in that availability much moves, much undoes and much is understood. You become un-blinded, you begin to clearly see and really open. You're a baby once again! Open, joyous, an outpouring - no longer a 'someone' but pure outpouring.

You will still be walking among the mixed conditioning of beings who don't know who they are. Here is a non-dual question for you: I am not asking you: "Do you know who you are? " No, this is a reverse question, "Do you know who they are? "

I am endeavouring to show you how vast you are. Much of existence is a mirror of the deeper realities. Maybe you only read a sense of self, person or a sense of 'other' and the world, but Awareness is that that pervades all that, is the ground of all that and makes all that possible.

The Point of Existence

Nothing-Aware reads 'a chair'. Nothing-Aware reads 'a door'. It is in the very ordinary. Nothing-Aware knows trees, flowers and birds. All this is being read by *What You Are* but it is also an appearance in *What You Are*. It is forming the moment of eternal Awareness.

Infinite Awareness, infinite conscious Awareness having immediate finite experience, moving in the mystery that I Am the totality of experience. Nothing-aware Knowing. It is the very ground of anything that could ever take place. Hence *you* are the continuum. You do not discontinue. Nothing is aware of the forms of this reality. Now read a little deeper, what does the flower mean for you? Is this a form of expression of a deeper flowering? Is the perfume the very essence of your being? Is the non-sense turning into sense?

In every manner and way, it doesn't matter whether it's a thought, a feeling, a sensation or an event, the light of meaning is shining. *You* are the streaming of this moment.

Where do you stream from? Where do you come from? You are traveling up the stream, which is forming the form. If you're only communing with the stream, then that is immediately the form. Come a little way up the stream, what is forming now has a different relationship. Keep coming up the stream into an ever finer relatedness. The more you travel up the stream, the more you see and know what moves you, has you and what you truly belong to.

If you don't travel up the stream you will have a shallow relatedness to this life, to *What You Are*.

If you do travel up the stream, you will come to a point where You poured out from. A miracle exists right there, the fact you have had life experience, means you have already gone beyond where you streamed out of.

Now you come from deeper in the realisation of Self, deeper than you have ever known. Knowing knows. Somehow you know a different kind of opening, movement and forming.

You are the new testament to the truth you move as the Self. You are the book of Life. You are the transcendental One. So, you exceed where you come from further up the waterfall of Love. It is the point of existence. You have a mirror to show you where you've come from. The forms of yourself demonstrate to you what you are being.

Read the moment deeply. Cease listening to the world, your self, your mind. It will only obey you 'being *You*'. If you're being 'two', a like and a dislike, it will obey

that and form that experience. If you are being
singularly true to the heart and deeper, then that will
come into form, but you *will* experience all the changes
on every level, to form that.

Day Four

*"Be open. Be so open that both negative and positive
disappear. That is the flowering of Love."*

The Body is a Genius Work of Love

Not so many realised beings speak about embodiment
and a new humanity. The body is not just chemistry
moving and to say that it is just made of Consciousness
is not enough. It is to understand how Consciousness
creates the body and how does the body move as
Consciousness? I will endeavour to keep turning you
inside out and keep touching on the deep and a deeper
knowing of what the body is; that the body is a
working, functional, manifest, genius work of Love.

Hormones are a Function of the Deep

I know a young girl, who is just moving through her
teenage years, just coming into being a young woman. I
hear people say around her: "She has hormones
moving", but hormones are a functionality of the deep.
More and more young people are going to experience
what is actually happening in their body and more and
more people will understand what the body truly is and
that the body makes physical where you are coming
from.

Hormones transport the energies of your intention and
your belonging because the unseen is destined to be
seen, to manifest. This is the outpouring. Whilst

Awareness experiences this conditional reality as a problem of my self, you will not understand that *you* are infusing your hormones with the problems of your self. `If we treat our life as something familiar the brain doesn't produce, let's just call it the 'spiritual' hormone. It can't, because the right key is not put in. The right key has to be turned, the key of deeper, higher belonging. The key that says: "It really doesn't matter how I feel in my sense of self, this thought and feeling doesn't tell me who I Am. Awareness knows it knows "I Am the I Am: The Self."

Most people that are awakening are still looking for comfort in their body-mind, mentally, emotionally, socially, psychically, in every way. You miss that the deeper touch of the presence of a deeper level opens an inner door and as Awareness you look into that door. You may open in your awareness a deeper sense of consciousness but you don't let it have your body, which basically means you don't let it have your full energy or pure sexuality. You are at a point where the door opened and a deeper level of the brain is ready to release a different, a spiritual hormone that will be the carrier of the deep, throughout the electro-magnetic circuitry that we believe is a physical body.

As that opens up, the full circuitry of the body-mind opens up to the deep and from that it is literally made physical. The hormone released from the deeper level of the brain from a deeper level of the being then opens and is able to transmit that throughout the physicality of the body. This is the embodiment of That that I Am. This is non-duality. The body-mind is a genius machine, a vehicle made from Love of Love.

Let's just go with the reflection of the young woman I spoke of, she is in this juxtaposition, this meeting of two rivers where there is the conditionality that says: "She has got hormones moving, every woman goes through this," but in an unspoken way, she will as Awareness be knowing something far deeper. She's in a point of two rivers; one old, quite polluted with conditional experiences of what sexual energy or embodiment is and one new which is the transformation of the body-mind from the higher dimensions opened. Awareness will be reading both rivers but only experiencing one which is the conditionality of every human being.

As Awareness, begin to understand that you read and open only as deep as you will allow. This world is teaching you to have comfort after comfort physically, mentally, emotionally, socially, religiously, in every possible way. You are looking for comfort, so when these two rivers meet you will refuse the new river because you are reading more of the difficult one because you are looking for comfort but not deeper Self-realisation. In looking for comfort you won't see the finest of the opportunity of the deeper awakening and the connection with the form that is an appearance in your awareness. You have form. You're actually the one that is evolving it not through something that you do, but by being deeply *What You Are*.

When your intention is to awaken deeper, the undoing of the old life, the old patterning will be moving in your usual sense of hormones but even more than prior to awakening. Because as soon as you're awakening the cup of the body-mind empties to have a deeper water of

life poured into it. The brain will have to produce a
higher frequency hormone able to manifest an all-
knowing, all-seeing, all-belonging to Oneness
body. Then there will be no difference between the form
and its formless interconnectedness. So your ability to
deeply awaken and stay in the alignment and the
presence of deeper Knowing and move that Knowing in
how you relate to the moment, amongst a body that's in
quite profound change, without needing comfort but
being wisdom, opens the deeper level of the brain that
creates the very fluid that is infused with the higher
dimensions and re-structures, re-wires the entire body-
mind instrument. This is a spiritual science, it's a real
science, it's the science of God.

It is essential in our awakening that we stay moving as
Truth-consciousness in body-mind displays of torrents
of terrible emotion and that we walk amongst that
conditional energy moving, but functioning from the
deeper realm that 'I' am realising. As Awareness you
must stay belonging to the deep.

The Feminine

You are taught that you are a woman and not a being
and not the Feminine Principle of the entire cosmos.
God as Feminine. Please hear the word 'Feminine' not in
the usual corrupt manner but as the power and energy
that manifests the forms of deeper reality. Where I come
from *She* is God as Feminine. I can't say, *She* is God as
'woman' for that is a form that passes away like man
does. *She* is a principle of Pure Consciousness with no
beginning and end.

Now I know I am 'Her', I know I am 'He' and I know I'm
'That' that seems to split into two but actually doesn't -
two principles of the One Self.

Only Being Does Doing

Only Being does the doing. When Awareness is Being;
Nothing-Aware being the Knowing, then it is the deep
that moves and does. It doesn't see something to change,
it just functions what It is. Change then is the
appearance of a deeper level. It is just the appearance of
the deeper level. It is not doing anything, it is just a
higher function.

Awareness having form begins to see a higher level
moving, functioning and the lower level changes by the
appearance of the higher level. Water is simply pouring.
It is simply pouring, but if I keep pouring that water I
will get wet feet! It will fill up the cup. Literally the old
will be as it were changed or emptied.

The pressure you feel in your body, the pressure you see
in this life is the awakening of the profoundly more
Real. It arrives and as it fills up this level, that that's not
the same vibratory tone feels the pressure of the
unknown. You can hear it complain, blame and scream
but it will soon be silenced by the movement of a
deeper, higher reality.

If you are awakening and sincere about it then you will
experience the pressure of the levels of self and person
that don't match the higher vibratory feel that's coming
in. The subconscious is emptying, the 'sub'-conscious,

underneath the Real. When there is no subconscious in the one who is listening to these words now, you will return as a child, in the innocence of your being, integrating in a pure form of body-mind. Like a child you will have no need to look at past experiences. You are the present experience of the brightness of purer reality, Awareness with no subject object is Oneness.

Keep The 'I' in Your Own Heart

Keep this 'where I come from' in your heart, not up on the throne over here… You are on the throne! Keep your eye in your own heart, then 'I' am the One seeing, knowing, moving. Sometimes you will have real clarity, equanimity, which means your whole body-being is in balance. Then there is an emptying, there is emptying, but you are in balance. Emptying is part of the spirit. Many passing visitors come through the House of the Beloved. Welcome them. You know they won't be staying long. If they stay they will be turning into 'I Am'. You *do* know this, really see it and live it, in short: love.

Arrows

Are your children your children? Are your friends your friends? Are your parents your parents? Or are they all arrows towards *What You Are*? Everything is an arrow pointing to 'I Am' - the Self. When you are true with this, any difficulty or discomfort on any level of body-mind doesn't point you away from your deeper Knowing, it points you *to* the response from your deeper Knowing, regardless of thoughts and feelings. That power opens the deeper level of the brain that transports that deeper power into the system of the body-mind, the hologram all the way into physicality. Spirituality is the instant form of 'I'.

If you react to repair some uncomfortable sense of self you will produce all the circumstances to hold on to a separate sense of self. It must happen because you are the Only One, so you are giving energy to the illusion of separateness. Give your power back to the deeper Knowing at the level of the heart. Have a sense of openness and softness with it, otherwise you will be moving your person to get this to happen and you will discover that doesn't work. It is the response as Awareness to deeper Knowing.

Two Rivers of Information

Often as Awareness, you are receiving two rivers of information: the familiar pattern of self emptying, and the quietness of the streaming of a finer level of Being.

If you are not truly sincere in awakening, you will simply listen to and give your energy to the pattern emptying. You will be integrating that for some time, so you go through another cycle of the return of that patterning and now it will be even more dense.

If you deeply say 'Yes', to your quiet Knowing, where you are knowing that on the level of the body-mind you can expect the self to be undoing but you remain true to the level you are moving in, that level will integrate.

This is the symbol of infinity, the subconscious patterning returning through the eye of the needle or the Knowing and the pouring in of a new dimension of reality, making physical the unseen. In that you'll be experiencing the metaphysical too, the in-between states as the higher dimension flows and turns into a level of forming. You'll be in the experience of the crossroads of the path going home and the new coming in.

It's really essential that you know this deeply. From that moment on, the hormones and the level of DNA and the level of the nervous system are moving in a finer vibratory essence, forming by the Creator, making real the Unseen into form.

Part of my work through *The Form Reality Practice* * is a demonstration of this, that Awareness awakening releases the functionality of the body-mind to the higher dimension of Knowing. You cease moving as a person and self with a past. You become the presence of Self realising Self forming. Your will has no idea about this... yet!

*B is the originator of The Form Reality Practice, a five-part movement sequence, taught on retreats with B and by teachers world-wide. The Form, is the manifest vehicle to integrate and embody everything B points to.

Timeless Awareness

What do we discover when we close our eyes?
This is what we discover: the basic space of Pure
Awareness.

When we open our eyes, what do we discover? We
discover that arising in that basic space in the timeless
Awareness, are the forms of Awareness, and the one
who is listening to these words *is* that space.

We open our eyes; phenomenal forms are appearing in
the basic space of timeless Awareness.

There is something missing though, for it is a Trinity.
What is missing is knowing Knowing.

How do you know the basic space of Awareness? How
do you know these forms, the light of which comes
from timeless Awareness knowing the Knowing?
The Self, knowing: 'I am aware Knowing, I have form
and knowing Knowing is the light of Awareness: the
Supreme Being.'

In the movement of The Form, that that is moving is
knowingly aware it knows. Timeless Awareness,
Eternity, your very own real presence. On this level of
timeless Awareness form presents itself to timeless
Awareness. In the deeper levels of timeless Awareness
subtle forms are moving, all being moved by and as
timeless Awareness. In short you do not die. Even more
so: only 'I' exist. The 'I' that's listening to these words
now. There's nobody here but 'I'.

Become Silent

When you become silent and you truly are rested in every moment, power is returned to your heart. It is silent power and its power is the bright presence of That that you already are. All moves just because you are knowing Knowing. You are your own fulfilment.

Streaming as a Being Manifesting

If you keep going back, you, the one who's listening to these words now, you will come to your original face which is the deep. Then (although there is no 'then' for it is not in time) expression will happen, a pin-prick of light which is the Self will fill perception for you are the Self: aware, fulfilled, free, and already complete.

You are going back into the stream of Being. How far up that stream can you move as Nothing-Aware?

Discover this whilst you have a body because it's all open for your realisation and the manifestation of those higher levels streaming. It will all manifest whilst you Awareness have a level of form.

It is paradoxical: what is then accomplished by nobody is a level of unseen bright Reality enabled to have form. It is an accomplishment by nobody for the one who is bringing it needs no accomplishment because it already is whole. It simply loves lovingly knowing What It Is.

From this place of placeless-ness the expanse of your original timeless Awareness is knowing and seeing All.

Love's Pouring

When the power of *What You Are* returns to your heart, you begin to see how much you give power to separate yourself. The more you see that and give that power back to the deeper Knowing through the heart centre, you begin to feel and know deep restedness. No matter how things appear, all is good. Power is returned to Being. Power not used as a separate sense of self equals the expansive space of Timeless Awareness.

When power moves from Being it is like a breeze. It comes from nowhere, moves into the All-ness and disappears into nowhere. This is the power of the presence of Love, and it is the one listening to these words now.

When you really see things 'as they are' you realise why you wanted to stay asleep, for it seems that your self is vulnerable when you are openness itself.
But you are not vulnerable, nothing can touch *What You Are*. You are Loves' pouring.

Day Five

"Whilst you have form, drink the love of Truth. Then the river flows."

Your Original Face

Let's look at the inner landscape. You miss it because
you project immediately out. Close your eyes and you
are there, gentle and open. Understand that your mind
doesn't prefer that 'nothing happening' place. Just close
our eyes, gently, gently soften and you won't project
onto the screen. Your body and all bodies are a
projection on to the screen. The screen *is* infinite
Knowing. It is that that you already are.

When a level of deeper reality moves, it comes from
'there' which it basically is 'here'. It is the face of the
deep, your original face and that face turns into the face
of the Self: bright Awareness. And within the radiance
of bright Awareness, infinite worlds without beginning
or end arise and that is Reality, multi-dimensional. As
Awareness-Knowing you are multi-dimensional but
Nothing-Aware Knowing is its totality and the self is
realising its totality.

Now open your eyes. You just moved at incredible
speed and formed yourself. You just moved like
…remember the 'outpouring of the baby'? Whatever
level you are coming from, you are forming that level.
At least this is the opportunity: to form the level of the
unseen.

When it appears that you were born, the level that you came from is the unborn. So the Being that you believe is a child is the unborn. The body-form is the first formation of the unborn state and the Beingness behind the body-mind formation is streaming the information of that level.

Information is not as we know it with our limited mind. It is levels of reality or omnipresence that permeate all experience, that can be contactable, communed with and communicated and your body is the communication of the unseen level you arrived from.

Most beings on this planet never fulfil the embodiment of the realm they have come from. Most stay within the psychic structure of the earth plain and never ascend beyond it. This is why if you go to the spiritualist church, Auntie Florence would be saying that she is still having tea in another realm and Uncle Bart is still having his cigarettes, because they have just moved one little speck beyond form. They are still in repetition. They will keep coming around and around and around. They still have the same opportunity as every being but within that repetition Awareness stops and questions 'What am I'? and the moment that question is deeply sincere the deeper level opens and invites that Being in.

Awareness must fulfil the level it is pouring from, because this formed level of reality, the body-mind and the brain are instruments of the function of the realms of Oneness. Because every being has its own will, until the one will is seen and given to, which is Self-realisation, the realising of Oneness. For any being that ever comes into human form, the brain can only supply the hormones of repetition, so wherever you are repeating an experience you are only accessing one level of deeper reality and only the same level of brain - it's called 'ground-hog day'! You are looping...

Whenever Awareness sees repetition, quieten and reach for the next level in. You will need to be living a much more heart-connected silent inner life. In having a busy interior you are missing all the doors, you are walking past doors that are awaiting your next walking into. You are too concerned with protecting your known sense of self so the brain can only secrete the hormones of familiarity. To reach the core of the brain where the pineal gland is, sometimes called the 'cosmic aerial' which connects every chakra with the One, you'll need to reach this deeper level.

Right now: relax, relax, gently, gently relax! It's like an inner sigh: "Aaaaahhhhh". You know when you've been working and you sit down and you believe it's the body relaxing, but it is actually Awareness letting go of controlling the body-mind. Awareness relaxes and sits in the seat of the Beloved. It's not just that your feet are off the ground, it's that all your forms have returned relating to the heart. They are at rest because you are not concerned about a separate sense of self. Then a deeper level of the brain opens which only opens for the deeper level of your being and it secretes a hormone chemical that's able to transport the deeper realisations and form them. This is why we do value the body because it's a psycho-spiritual, energetic sound system, moved by and *as* the light of Awareness.

If you are just reading human conditionality you have no access to this, you're not putting the key in, you're not unlocking the mystery of You. You have no ability to do it. It is like a safety lock because if you open it and you're not ready for it, it will be far too much for you. It always comes at the right time. But then when the right time comes you put a time delay on it because you look in your history book of 'me' and it tells you this is not the right time and you believe it. Well actually you don't believe it but you side with it. It's easier to side with it but then you miss the opportunity that this life brings to you, which is not only to realise the Self, but to manifest the way of the Self in the human body. You are manifesting this moment *now*. Realise and realise how this is taking place. Be the Love master of your universe.

Drink the Love of Truth

There is so much information in the Awakening field about 'detachment'. You must be 'detached'. Well, I don't believe that. This is not detachment. It's having the love to know this, having the nerve to know, having the love to know who 'I Am'. Detachment is dry. Try to drink detachment. You're drinking sand! You're in the desert. Whilst you have form, drink the love of Truth. Then the river flows. Detachment then turns into wisdom; a pure way of Being.

Then there is not so much 'detachment'. It is the gentled way of your being. It is an ocean and there are streams of it.

Look at all the beautiful streams here! Just look into each other's eyes, which is the same as saying look into each other's hearts. Streams flowing from the same ocean. Fear falls away. There are no others but there is Being individuated; wisdom's river flowing in which we know love.

Now when that comes into the body-mind, the manifestation is our pure sexuality moving. The energy of our movement as the Being moving in existence to the body-mind, that energy manifests the one good life and it's known and experienced within. It comes up within. It is un-missable when the deep moves. It only comes by invitation though. You need to write your invitation card. The letterbox is your heart and the way in which you move from within.

Respond always a little deeper and a little deeper, move ever deeper inside. You have been believing you are moving as a thought or a feeling but you are a being moving inside. When you move deeper you'll move the deep up to the surface, despite the old movements of the sense of self up on the surface. Abide in your heart and you will come to a living understanding of the undoing of the patterning in the sense of self and person and even in the world. Why is this? It is supposed to undo, because if it didn't, the forms and sense perception would still represent the past and not represent and form the presence of your new deeper awakening and movement. For you are here to work out into form what you are being and knowing in the deep.

Crete Retreat

*"Awareness, you are finding your way,
not home in the distance, but home in the Now,
home in this moment of presence,
unpatterned, unfamiliar,
untouched."*

Day One

"You are freedom itself. To be free you need to be letting go of what defines you on the surface. Everything on the surface needs to be set free, so the un-definable You can move through what you used to think you were."

Finding the Way

Discover the presence that you are. Amongst that presence, the beingness of presence, you may begin to discover that you are entering the body-mind right now.

In our current societies, our cultures, friends and families, we are constantly informed of a pattern rather than of 'finding the way'. There is no problem with that. It is all mirrors. We meet many difficulties as we find the unpatterned way, as we discover not to identify with the felt pattern along with its thought. Levels of patterning that have been identified with by Awareness, that is 'you and I', are constantly throwing up stories and information. We are in a massive informational field but that informational field is a tiny dot in what one is.

This is not a concept, it is Love.

Find the way of softening and opening. In the deepening of that openness, as Awareness appearing to be a person, you are dropping into the unformed levels of your wholeness, because in the deep you are complete.

You are dropping into deeper levels of wholeness that are unlike anything you would relate to on the surface through thoughts and feelings and movement of mental, emotional, psychological and physical experience. It is not made of matter, although matter is made of You, Awareness. It is not made of the elements, although the elements are made of You, Awareness.

Awareness, you are finding your way, not home in the distance, but home in the *now*, home in this moment of presence, unpatterned, unfamiliar, untouched.

The unseen You is the pressure you feel on your familiar known patterned way. For the deep, unpatterned, unfamiliar and already complete, does not mix with the familiar. It doesn't mix. The mixing only happens because of the power and ability of Awareness to mix the surface levels, rather like a paint palette.

As Awareness comes up into sense of self and person, this biological micro-computer moves as soon as you press the command button and on the screen, forms of unpatterned Awareness arise, mixed with the conditional level of patterns, identified with since apparent birth.

This is our ability on the surface of the body-mind, to mix what we have experienced in a linear manner of past with what we are awakening to, that has no past. Awareness can mix this on the surface. It basically gets mixed up and it gives itself permission to be mixed up. As Awareness awakens to what it is, it unmixes this level of reality by staying true to the heart of Knowing.

That is why life gets so terribly difficult when you are awakening.

All the pressures you see in the world, all the pressures you feel in this life are your endeavour to unmix reality on this timeline of belief that you are a body-mind and you have had a past.

Whether we know it or not, we are already complete, endeavouring to give expression to our completeness, not through familiarity or the belief that we are a body-mind. If there is a 'learning' then maybe it is the learning to forgive ourselves for getting so mixed up and reveal the heart to the heart.

However your life is right now, is the place of discovery.

Deeper than the Patterned Sense Of Self

It takes a tremendous amount of energy to stay present in a human body as Pure Awareness or innocence. But you did it when you were very young because you had not as yet identified as a body-mind form. The truth is we don't exist. Only 'I' exist, 'I', the one listening to these words now.

Awareness moves, 'I' takes place, in other words there is Knowing. Knowing moves its radiance and the elements make form of that.

When you move deeper than the patterned sense of self, you empty the patterned sense of self. When you move a little bit deeper, what you have been knowing on the surface vibrates. That vibration, when you are open, is the replacement of the forming you are familiar with. It is the deep moving to meet you coming in, a union point of the same one meeting itself. It can be challenging to your sense of self, or another's sense of self because you are rebuilding your sense of self to match what you are awakening to.

Faith

Faith is knowing you know deeper than any experience you have in the body-mind. It is Knowing. It is not objective. As you move into the Knowing, you read beyond sense-perception. All difficulty, pain and distraction is in your incomplete self, not in You. You are deeper than the body-mind. You got used to believing you are a 'someone'. As you drop your name, drop the familiar, levels in the body-mind that you patterned as false security, you will begin to feel them dismantle by you realising deeper. There is no need of security anywhere in Reality, which is in You. To realise that and live that is the living of You in the body-mind. You are rebuilding the body-mind as a being.

The Genius of Life One Is

If you leave your self alone, you will come into your first fear: being alone. If you continue to leave your self alone, you come into the freedom of 'being aloneness'. Then on the surface, you will realise All-Oneness. It keeps on unfolding and growing in this way. The deeper you go, the more will take place on the surface because now you are moving at a speed that is incomprehensible to what you believed you were. You will discover you instantly know. You realise the genius of life one is, but there is no one there knowing it. It is just Knowing that is knowing.

Take Out the Concept of Love

If you struggle with conceptual love, you will feel the struggle of all your forms endeavoring to relate to your heart as Love. Take out the concept of Love, see that you are the movement of all forms *as* Love and you will cease struggling. The struggle is You separating You into parts when You are the whole.

Day Two

"The Reality you are searching for
is not distant, it is right now.
The Goodness you are seeking is right now.
It has never gone anywhere.
It is not in the future, it is not in the past.
This living essence, this living Goodness is now.
It is nowhere else."

Passing Through the Dark as the Light of Awareness

Within the retreat, Awareness discovers its own bright reality, demonstrating the illusion that we are separate and revealing our core beliefs sustained by our belonging to the world and not to what we deeply are.

Often these levels come up pretty fast, in the first minutes, hours or days. What we then do is we use our established coping mechanisms to cope with what is coming up. When patterns are moving, you head to consult your sense of self as if it were your agony aunt. You go and sit at the feet of ignorance, at the feet of arrogance, at the feet of that that *cannot* know *What You Are*, yet *is* made of *What You Are*; it's a paradox.

When you are passing through what we call darkness, core beliefs arising in your awareness, they will be appearing through what you call 'my life'. They appear through your patterned thoughts and feelings. Consulting your feelings is not the way. The way is the one who is listening now, listening to what 'I' is. That is the way, the only way.

Passing through the darkness shows you have not integrated your being as much as you have integrated your sense of self. You have integrated 'What about me?' instead of 'Who I Am'- Consciousness itself, or 'What I Am'- Awareness itself, which are arrows to the depths of Reality.

What I Am or Who I Am is not consulted by your self but is direct and in immediate Knowing. It is superfast, the highway of Reality and it wakes up and wakes down, wakes in and wakes out.

When core beliefs begin to move, you are going to discover your attachment to how you think, how you feel and how you relate to the illusion that you are a someone. This is brilliant! It is a moment of pure release into profound but simple openness, because all this is taking place in a vast spaciousness of what Awareness is, the one who is listening to these words now. It is a pin-prick. That is how small all this that is going on is. It seems so big to your identification with the forms you use to tell yourself what you are, instead of knowing directly 'What I Am'.

This is only living in you by you *being* this knowledge. If you are not being it, in preference of thoughts or feelings, then the deeper realisation cannot move. It is moved by your relatedness to the deep and in relating to it you are waking up and also waking deeper down until there is no waking up or waking down.

We will look into this more as we move on; the realising of *what* I am which then reveals in life *who* I am. Awareness: what. Consciousness: who. The what moves in the who. In moving in the who, the what discovers what it is, the who discovers where it comes from, and it is the same One realising it is total.

The Illusion

The body-mind is not an illusion. The illusion is the patterned core belief that Awareness has brought into the body-mind. That is the only illusion, handed down from father to son, mother to daughter. It is like that. No one is to blame because your father is not your father and your mother is not your mother.

Day Three

"Bliss, true happiness, is not derived from forms of experience but is actually what one IS."

Fasting on the Light of Love And Knowing

When you think you are a body-mind, to fast on the light of Love and Knowing is quite difficult. Fasting is not 'not eating'. Fasting is not eating from the tree of separate sensed self. That puts you in the tree of life because that is *What You Are*, inside and outside, rooted in the tree that is Thee.

Your First Body

If you only identify with what you know you to be within the heart, you will realise the entire universe is your first body formed. You become open to the mystery of the adventure of realising 'What I Am', what truly is and the disentanglement of identification with the form, which sets the form free to be what one is.

The Form Reality Practice is simply that. It points to that in movement.

Formless Levels of Knowing
The Form Reality Practice

What seems to be part of the body is an energetic,
electromagnetic circuitry in which Awareness-Knowing
is manifesting the human, to fully embody divine or
Pure Being embodied. For this to come through, forms
appear to be solid but are actually all open.

When we move in The Form, although it looks like
from the outside you are looking at someone who has
form, from the inside it is the movement of Awareness
awakening to levels of Knowing.
It is the movement of Awareness awakening to *formless*
levels of Knowing.

Every movement that appears to be a shape, is an
entrance to a frequency of one's own being. Every
movement that appears to be a shape, such as a hand or
a foot, an eye or a toe, a building or a walk, a yes or a
no, is either an entrance into mind, on a patterned level,
or an entrance into your Being.

As you practice, the entrance into your being opens the
form, the expression that forms what appears to be a
body. Behold it with your heart, with your original
spaciousness.

Naturally, there will be a level of you grasping hold of
what you believe is familiar, like when you look in the
bathroom mirror. There is also a deeper level of you,
knowing the Knowing of Awareness and it moves. And
that really is not only the movement of your body or
your mind, or even the pumping of the heart; that's the

movement of the universe. The movement of Knowing, moving as Love.

Notice the movement you are beholding with your awareness placed only at your heart. Whilst you have a body, a heart full of Knowing, it is a body full of Love. You are knowing the frequencies of the presence of the movement of life.

Here it looks like someone *doing* something. Within the human field of manifestation, the hands, the feet, the body and all that seems to be material is a movement of Awareness. Awareness knowing it knows manifesting the pattern of what is 'human' in the endeavour to come all the way up into the moment of forming as Awareness in the Being that is doing. It is Being that is doing, there is no doer. The Beingness is the doing.

Day Four

"Making experience 'mine' is the beginning of all difficulty.

The Moment Awareness Identifies With Experience

As a child, we were taught to identify with experience. Awareness zoomed into experience and made it 'mine'. When you were very young, there was just wide open experience; the whole of life being one singular movement, not in bits, not in parts but the simple joy of wide open Being moving in forms of Being.

The moment Awareness identifies with an experience it likes or dislikes, which is the conditional nature on this level until Awareness awakens to what it is, then Awareness in existence evolves its Knowing and develops its forms within its perception.

The moment Awareness identifies with experience, it zooms into that experience, singles it out from the sun rising, from the moon rising, from the stars shining, from the waves moving, from the birds singing, from the owl in the night, from the breeze, from the wind, from the smell of the earth, from the movement of all life. It singles out the total experience of 'I Am' and makes a single moment of experience 'mine'...Difficulty begins right there, suffering begins right there.

Day Five

*"Your only experience is:
I am knowingly aware I am Awareness,
that in which the universe forms
and moves and dissolves
in my return to the Deep,
to the Source that I Am."*

Excursion to the Cave of Zeus

The 'Prior To'...

The cave represents the 'prior to', the void. That is why
people retreat to a cave, to come to the real Self. There
you discover the mind stops. You find there is no
substance in the cave. It is pure and clear Awareness.
This is where it all begins and all ends, in You.
When you come out of the cave you walk in the forms.
All the stones you walk on are what you individuated
and separated. You are passing through these stones for
the transformation of form in your new bright
Awareness.

Day Six

*"Let the knowledge of freedom mean more to you than
the feeling of freedom."*

Pure Speaking, Pure Listening

The speaker can only point and the listener can only
listen. The speaker can point to where the pointing is
coming from. When the speaker lets go of the need to
point as a someone, someone is on the decrease and
Awareness is on the increase, is deepening. When the
listener is listening because the listener can only listen,
then the listening comes from the 'unlistening' to the
stories of a separate sense of self. It is the process of
'unlistening' from the point of view of someone.
Listening becomes pure.

Then the one who is pointing and the one who is
listening realise they are the same one. Both pointing
and listening disappear and only Awareness remains.
Pure Awareness, which is Love, remains.

When Awareness moves up into the level of form, the
one who is pointing will endeavor to point from a place
never pointed to before. That is his appointed function.
The one who is listening will listen from what they have
never heard before. That is their appointed function.
There they find they are the same one discovering who
this 'I' is, this ability to be conscious - deeply, wholly
and utterly. They are what all this arises in, the
Awareness that makes all this possible.

One Taste

When by grace we have a taste - one taste only, we taste how Being moves, how Being functions, what Being is, what Being does that makes everything whole.

It does not divide. It moves in every level of a human life exactly as what it is. This raises a function of a level to a movement of Being. Pure Being let loose in the movement of a human life is nothing other than glorious. It is pure Love.

Awareness realises in its utter giving away the forms that it has separated from its true Knowing, its being. It sees how function happens quite naturally in the mobility of being true to heart Knowing.

Being does not use a thought. Being does not use a feeling. Being does not seek out a particular thought or feeling 'to have' as opposed to another thought or feeling 'not to have', a particular person to meet, a particular person not to meet. It meets everything as its unchangeable Self, its unchangeable Beingness.

When Awareness begins to awaken to its heart and to belong to its being, this allows the streaming of Being to have all the forms that Awareness has separated into like and dislike, good and bad, right and wrong. This also allows Being to move into any energy centre, to be completely in it and change it just by *being* in it. That centre then begins to vibrate at the frequency of Being, emptying out all the forms or energies of preference and opening up the deeper realms within the earth, the deeper realms within the unseen. They marry, which means they merge. This merging is Oneness moving, giving Awareness the ability to be completely moved by its own Love, direct and immediate.

Mobile in its own Love even amongst what it once used to identify with. Breaking open everywhere within its experience. Breaking open in its mind, breaking open in its heart, breaking open in its feeling, breaking open in its relationships.

Awareness becomes mobile and stabilised in the deeper truth it is belonging to, realigning the whole body-mind with the light of its own Love.

In such a giveaway to its being, Awareness is home amongst the debris of the separation it imposed on itself and it is able to function from the deeper levels of realisation, in amongst the old functionality falling to pieces. In this, Love shines through the knowing of the love of oneself; the Self or Pure Being.

Day Seven

*"Let go of moving as someone. Simply move as a Being
- totally subjective to what the heart is. No objective.
Discover how that relates to everyday movement. You
are entering the alchemist."*

Love's Outpouring

The unseen can be termed to be *new* in your experience
as Awareness, when you touch upon what is deeper than
your personalised experience and you touch upon it,
completely open to losing everything that you have
experienced as 'you'.

You are now available to be filled up by the deeper
touch of your own original being and your own original
being finds you all open. It moves up into that openness
and you remember *What You Are*, its goodness and its
purity. The newness is bright, simply because you have
surrendered everything. Every idea that you have ever
had, every experience you have ever had. You have
surrendered so completely open that everything can be
filled by your original nature. That is the movement of
profound Love, profound sweetness.

Everywhere you turn with that pouring in inside,
outside is being filled by that Love. Everywhere you
turn will be filled by that Love. You look at a neighbour
and that Love will fill up your neighbour. That Love
will fill up the sky. That Love will fill up everything

you could possibly ever know or look at. Everything. *That* is what you love.

You are able to move into the streaming of the Love outpouring. You are able to move into the dimensions of other levels where this one Love is pouring, making everything one. You are able to flow upstream and come to a level unspeakably profound. You are so available in this life, so opened, no longer needing to register an experience. You now have right of way in the stream to the ocean of Love, because you have given up all identification with experience. Now you can go up river into the higher streams. Whilst you have a body it is formed right here right now, in this form and the form is made new. The form sings the new, but you are still travelling, as it were, and realising *What You Are*. Never were you anything other than this but the one and only constant that is, realising what It Is and being it. That is the sweetness that you are touched by, your original freedom. You are no longer your own. It becomes clear to you that you belong only to this.

To be where you are now coming from whilst having form means that the forms of experience will move, because on this level you are the whole body but also a cell within it. There will be an influence of the cell you are, within the whole body you are.

An entirely new human is coming into being, a field that is not dependent on forms of experience but a field that is an outpouring of original Love. In that moment, you stream that original Love by coming from it. More and more doors open and the delight of your being is what you know you belong to.

Day Eight

The Untangling of Experience

When Being moves because Awareness is belonging to it, it fills up all spaces you could possibly ever see and know. You look at something and it fills it up. You think something, it fills it up. You feel something, it fills it up. Wherever you look, your being fills it up with what Love is, an extraordinary movement of Being. You cannot make this happen. Mostly you have suffered for it. One master said, 'you have to suffer *rightly'*, which means know what pain is about. Clearly know what it is about.

For some all this remains conceptual, just words: " a movement of Being that is profoundly real…" because Awareness objectifies everything. Then there is subject and object, but that is not the truth. That is the split that Awareness is doing in identification with the experience of objects. But there is no experience of objects, there is only 'objects arising as one form', like the universe. Objects arising as one form within pure knowing Awareness. Pure knowing Awareness is the totality of experience – whole, not two, not separate.

Objects arise in *What You Are*, they are made of *What You Are*. They come with you, because they *are* You formed.

Then there is a movement of Being when Awareness moves. It is no longer looking at an object. It is the movement of Awareness in Being that is the one and only constant: Love that is pouring.

This is a powerful moment because as Awareness untangles itself from objectifying, it no longer has any need to experience objects to know its own Love. This is Being. This is the true life, the one goodness, filling up the space that was once taken up by identification in separate sensing.

This cannot be done by a separate sense of self but by Awareness seeing very clearly that it is misidentifying with experience. The experience truly is 'I Am knowingly aware'. That is the sensation in the body, the deep sense that all is good, the deeper sense that everything is moving as it should, everything is calling as it does and I have this deeper calling to know more of 'What I Am'.

Deeper Seeing and Knowing

Any pain is really pointing to an unseen level opening, to be filled up by your response to the unseen level. This is actually rebuilding the body, the mind, the person and the sense of self. There is a goldenness about this, when the purer energy that belongs to your Being arises.

Your being activates the purer energy that comes up, just by you as Awareness being aware of what is deeper. As you move in this life then and you are not moving in a robotic fashion but in utter openness, that gives way for the deeper levels to emerge.

Begin to see as the light of Love the possibility of deeper seeing and Knowing and what is really opening within. See how it does match a level of disentanglement to particular forms, mental, emotional wrapped in the movement of the body-mind, your humanness. When you let go of a level, you completely surrender because you see this is an old way and you look deeper and respond to the deeper level. This gives that level permission to come up and fill up the vacant space of that that you once moved in.

Discernment in Awakening

The 'I' of the knowing of Awareness is the brightness you really are. Discern *What You Are* from the sensations separated from Knowing in the streaming of life, the streaming of the moment. You *are* the light that is streaming.

Discern between the forms Awareness is disentangling and the deeper level of Knowing. Bring that together by speaking directly of life *as it is*. As you look at life as it is, disentangle your aware Knowing from the attachment to particular experiences by aligning with the deeper unseen level of you that is awakening.

Dive Right in
The Form Reality Practice

The practice of The Form is the same as your everyday
life but in your everyday life you don't always look to
what is deeper than how you usually function.

You are trained to keep things the same, rather than
introduce what you are moving from as a being in a new
way. You won't know how that looks until you go there.

Within The Form you can either move in form attached
to what your mind thinks is a structure or you can move
in form formlessly, unidentified with the body-mind, its
thoughts, its feelings and its concepts.
You can dive right in.

Day Nine

"Care for yourself on such a deep level that it is not about any emotion, it is about Truth, the power of Truth, which is real Love."

Undoing Your Old Ways

You are remaking your interior by not believing you have an exterior. When you have pain, when you are suffering, that is your attachment to past experience. You do not suffer when you have released past experience in the light of knowing what you deeply know is true that you are awakening to.

Pain will remain until it doesn't. It does its work. There is much work going on in pain. Leave that pain alone. Don't put it onto others. Don't believe it is 'you' but do acknowledge there is pain. Within that pain there is an unconsciousness you are making conscious, a return of that energy to the bright energy of Love meeting the bright energy of Knowing, reforming this level of reality.

Energy or pure sexuality will follow you wherever you go and form what you believe in. Remain true to what you are awakening to and most definitely all the patterns of egoity will empty out. You will experience that energy moving in the body-mind in many different ways, undoing your old ways so that you may know your old ways more cleanly, more wholly. You forgive yourself for moving in such a way. Now you know clearly this is not the way of your being.

Be true to the depths of your Knowing. Be one with
Knowing. That is being one with your Self, deep
Knowing, not mental or emotional experiences, which
are your familiar forms. Recognise your usual forms,
they are like an old friend. Then you will know the
unusual Awareness you are now in.

Day Ten

"When you realise no one owes you anything,
nor does the cosmos, then you are
going to become more naked, open and free,
to discover directly this powerful and yet gentle Love
which is your true nature.
You might not be used to such straightness,
but here it is in the name of Love."

Keep Yourself Unblinded

Q: *I saw something today, something that I have created. It was revealed after a certain amount of contemplation. What I created was a puppet and it had the kind of characteristics of a voracious predator. When I looked, when I finally regained enough presence of mind to see what I had done and what this entity was, it was like a black hole. It was at the same time nothing as well as all-devouring in terms of Awareness. My knowledge is that what this thing is has no reality. It is something that I have cultivated and fed consciously and unconsciously. Whatever feelings I have about it, I know that it is not me, it is something that I can either work to release or to just blindly accept.*

B: Blindly accept what, the whole thing?

Q: *Yes*

B: Well, obviously you're not blind any more.

Q: *No, I'm not..*

B: So, you can't blindly accept it, you can now consciously …

Q: *Yes! (laughs in recognition)*

B: There you are, so that got rid of the *blind* bit. You can no longer say "Oh I didn't see that", because you do see it.

Q: *I do see it, yes.*

B: It's you as Awareness that is seeing it. We can pretend we are 'someone' but really you are Awareness. All the power that is of Awareness then can maintain that and you're just making a huge burden for yourself at some point in this life. By unblinding yourself, which you have just done and then ignoring it, you are going to create your own suffering because now you really have the power to make it much more solid. And yet something says you have a greater knowledge, that what you are seeking is already *What You Are*. It's not a question of 'will you accept it?' Isn't it a question of you being unblinded now? You're not blind anymore. You do see.

Q: *I do see, yes.*

B: "I once was blind but now I see," says a very wonderful song. Do you prefer being blind, or do you prefer to see? That's how it is. Of course, there are many who prefer being blind. See what you are really called to.

You are called to really see. Then it costs you all those games, because they are of no value anymore and you are called to realise Love as yourself.

Recognise that what you truly value is a power beyond belief. Now you can see when you're giving away power to what you see you created and you made yourself blind to. To return that power to your awakening is pretty powerful and to stay with it is real. It will change your life like you have never known before.

In giving power to what your heart really is, you won't need illusions any more. You won't need to protect anything anymore because you're unveiling your heart to you and the entrance to *What You Are*. Value that.

Give that energy to being unblinded, because the manner in which you unblinded yourself to that activity means you're really moving to unveil You to You! Use that energy to unveil more and unveil more. Realise that you are bright freedom, you don't need to play any more games. Should you play games now that you're unblinded, you're going to wind them together much more forcibly. Why would you want to do that? What you seek is *What You Are*, so why not head straight home?

You have unblinded yourself. That's pretty powerful. It means there is Love on the move in you. There is a new light, a new cleanliness, because you have unblinded your heart. Keep yourself unblinded. Return home. Discover the Good, which is what you are. You are of incredible value to this earth, and to this universe.

Never underestimate what you bring, as a human being, to another's life and to the whole planet.

The Undoing As Pure Self Awakens

In ordinary everyday reality people, ordinary everyday people like you and I, often go through processes of which they have no real understanding. They have no idea of what is really happening, that their pure Self is awakening within their own consciousness and is undoing patterns of egoity, patterns of want, patterns of need, mentally, emotionally, and definitely sexually, because that is the stuff which builds the universe of Consciousness into forms of the universe.

People go through marriage breakups, all sorts of relationship breakups but they don't complete the process. Very few human beings truly complete a process on any level of energy, any level of enlightenment of a centre, all the way through.

What we do is, we go through a difficult time emotionally and because we've identified emotion to be Love, which it is not, we feel sorry for ourselves instead of caring for ourself on such a deep level that it is no longer about emotion, it is about Truth, the power of Truth, which is real Love.

We go through stuff and we think of it as: 'someone's left me' or 'someone's unkind to me or, 'that's a shame' whereas it is none of that. It is that all this is being called to realise the Self. Even a blade of grass is. That's what's going on.

Someone leaves someone and they may have emptied out a level of emotion but it's still active, it is still activating in the world. Then these two go in search of comfort somewhere. They look for someone who is going through the same process, so they can comfort each other. The higher centres are shut in this, particularly the heart centre. Some even make this a new partnership and it is not a real partnership. It has no real value in it. It just holds you back from realisation in this lifetime. I am not against this, I am just pointing to the unreality of it.

There is an immense power at work here that you can divert to keep a few centres that are undoing because your being is awakening in your awareness. You can stop the process fully happening and use this energy to partner up with someone else. You actually think that something real is going on but you are just having more comfort for a few years until you find that this is not going to work. The whole fighting game starts just like it did every time with everyone else. You haven't gone through the door yet. You are not that deeply true yet.

What You Are Cannot Break

Let the brokenness be known, let the brokenness happen. You are going to find sweetness in the brokenness. When you are really broken, all that can break is what you are not. *What You Are* cannot break and it shines through. See what is opening up in you. See what is coming out of the cracking, what is inside the cracking, rather than the experience of cracking.

Nothing in the Way

B: What calls you to this retreat?

Q: *The Self-realisation of Being, eternal freedom*

B: What stands in the way of the Self-realisation of Being? What stands in the way that?

Q: *My old self, my old patterns.*

B: Ok, are you ready for this? Nothing stands in the way. That is the answer. How can anything stand in the way of eternity? How? Nothing stands in the way. It is a belief, an empowered belief that you create Awareness, and put in the way. It is called mind. Nothing stands in the way of Self-realisation. Nothing. Just the illusion of belief that you are separate, that you are a body-mind. Nothing stands in the way.

Realise whether you are soaking up your little self and looking for support for your little self. Your heart, even just the tiniest little drop of your heart, is more than enough to support an eternity of selves. But you have to come. You consult your sense of self and your sense of experience. You constantly do, so you constantly move away from what you really are, and yet you don't because you can't, because you are the Self, aware and knowing. You build an illusion based around dual experience.

Q:*(Laughs and laughs...)*

B: Your laughter is emptying out the duality, the illusion that experience is what you are. Nothing stands in the way, only what you Awareness put in the way, because you *are* the way.

Just come towards your heart, just a little, and then totally belong to that little that you open in your heart. You will find your heart opens and responds to you giving all that you are to that tiny little opening.

This is not to get away from your sense of self, because that will still be functioning in the way you put it together. Instantly belong to what you deeply know is true and you will begin to function from that level, amongst the dysfunction of how you used to move and operate. Now a new functionality, an enlightened Awareness begins to move as You.

The Loss of the Drama

If you look, your only pain is believing you are limited. Your pain is believing that your self and its experience of duality has anything to do with what you really are. It doesn't. You have been taught that and you have loved the play and the drama of that. The play of that is giving you self-identification and the loss of that drama is quite a lot for you, because you have been enjoying it for so long and investing much in the drama. If you don't have enough drama, you will need to go and make some more. Very few people understand the quiet nature of the immediacy of aware Knowing. It is profound but the profundity doesn't open up until you stay one with it.

Lift Yourself Up!

Lift yourself up, this not an instruction, it's a pointing. Lift your self up. Lift yourself up with your heart. Lift yourself up. If you are sloppy anywhere, lift yourself up. If you are lazy anywhere, lift yourself up. Care for yourself in the nature of being true. Lift it up. Raise it up. Then it starts to know *What You Are*, otherwise it believes it is you.

Day Eleven

"An infinite movement in a finite moment
is You pouring Love into form.
As it pours over, it blesses everyone.

No one is doing the blessing,
no one is doing the pouring.
Aware Knowing, knowingly aware
is action without someone behind it.

All one vast movement of Being.
It is aware, it is knowing and it can individuate into
droplets of unique experience of 'I Am'."

Honesty is the Key, Honesty to Knowing

If you want to find out what's holding in your body,
have a look what is holding in your life. What is holding
in the life is what is holding in the body, what is holding
in the body is holding in the life and what is holding it
is Awareness.

That is how you can as Awareness see, that what is
locked in your body is already appearing in your life.

See that what your body is made of is made of that
which the stars shine in, the sun shines in, the moon
rises in, the rain rains in, the clouds move in, the
mountains are in. Become that honest and address life
from an honest heart-knowing. Honesty is the key,
honesty to Knowing.

Knowing is pure aware Consciousness. Get *that* honest.
You could even realise the Self, the radiance one truly
is. It is all dependent on how deep Awareness will dive
into its pure Knowing, instead of attributing its
Knowing to life experience.

Wider and Deeper than the Room.

Patterns will toss and throw you around.
Only so you can know yourself.
Who knows how long that might take?
It could take one tiny fragment of a second.
The question is, are you ready for infinite Knowing to
replace your finite forming?
That is the kind of Love that you are remembering you
deeply are.

Build a sense of self and person,
from infinite Knowing, direct and immediate.
Cease comparing the Knowing with the experience
within the sensation in the mental body or emotional
body.

Respond to the infinite Knowing
regardless of the separate sensing of experience...
Rest all your forms into the heart's Knowing,
yearning to realise Itself.

See wider and deeper than the room.
Soften wider and deeper than the room.
Open wider and deeper than the experience.
Unusual experience will open.
It won't belong to a somebody.

Move into the Unseen
The Form Reality Practice

In the movement of The Form, move into the
invisibility of your Knowing.

Realise Awareness, the invisibility of your Knowing,
the unseen-ness of it.

It does not have a centre. It is Love.

Move into the invisibility of it, the transparency of it. It
is a direct communication of what already is the truth
that I am speaking of - daily life. It comes from the
realisation of the One *as* the One and is the One
moving.

All levels within the One move within the movement of
Reality Practice. So, as Awareness, you move in the
practice and you become opened.

You move into the unseen.

You are reforming your relationship with ignorance.
You are reforming the relationship with the deep.

Day Twelve

"You have all had experience of awakening, that is unquestionable, but are you still questioning who You are? 'That' is the question."

Infinite Knowing in Finite Form

To form *What You Are* and know the form of *What You Are*, you are having to fall out of infinite Knowing.

It is like a betrayal. That is why sometimes we feel ashamed to awaken; it is like we betrayed our infinite God or Good but we have not. It betrays its Self to realise what it is, because there is only this One.

To have a finite form is to fall out of infinite Knowing until one is ripe enough to be the infinite Knowing in a finite form.

You have to give up the objectification and the containing of power for someone who does not actually exist. Only the Self or 'I' exist.

You Are On Your Own Leash

Realising means to know 'What Is'. Realising also means to see 'what you give power to'. Power never has and never will belong to a body-mind identity. It all belongs to what you are as Being or aware Knowing. This power belongs to Awareness but it comes from the

Knowing or the Beingness that is pouring out of
Awareness.

Like a waterfall, Awareness is able to be aware in any
level of the outpouring but it can realise the total
outpouring and the source of that outpouring, which is
immediate bright Knowing that fills the perception.
Power then is pouring out of Awareness and fills the
perception of the one who is aware.

Awareness through Knowing direct, becomes absolutely
aware of the one and only outpouring, which is the light
of Awareness.

Awareness, like water pouring down a mountainside or
like a cup of water spilling on the ground, can know
every level of that pouring.

What is available to you as Awareness knowing the
light of Knowing, are the levels in which Pure
Awareness is pouring and streaming levels within the
reality of the one who is listening to these words now.

In existence that has you Awareness aware of yourself,
knowing yourself; this human self. It has you aware of
the human self without the need to register the
experience of self - 'small self'. You can register 'small
self' but you don't have to function from its conditional
information.

Habitually this is exactly what you do. You register
power being poured on this human level of forming self
and person. You register self-experience, which turns
into self-importance. The moment self-experience

moves, it registers in the body-mind and you immediately go to it because you are on its leash. You are so identified with it that its power moves you. You do not move it. You are pulled by it to protect it and live its insistence on keeping the power to itself.

The moment there is a deeper opening, unless you fully belong to it, you also register what takes place in deeper Knowing in the body-mind and you will run towards it, for it pulls you like a dog on a leash. You run to protect it and to make sure that it is not touched by the depth of the unknown Beingness, which is the one who is listening to these words. It is just unseen, unformed.

You run to protect it and it will speak through you and it will move you. This is not a problem but it is a problem to you who is bright shining free Awareness, pulled like a dog on a leash to protect the power you have given to a sense of self that is an illusion in that it is not *What You Are*. You are Love itself you are freedom itself, you are wholeness itself. That level of you is a living moving experiment. That is why we call it 'experience' or experiential. It is your growing ability to be *What You Are* in the experiential self.

Only in being *What You Are* and deeply belonging to the truth within and yet beyond your heart, the experiential self aligns with *What You Are* as a living way of Being in Truth.

True forms then are a living experience of Oneness. Awareness then no longer runs like a dog on a leash to the experience of self mentally, emotionally,

psychologically or in any relationship. It no longer
needs to defend its right to hold power in separation.

In truth only 'I', this Love that is listening to these words
now, exist. Nothing else exists but 'I'. Everything is
made of 'What I Am', this aware Knowing. You fall out
of infinite Knowing to form finite form of the infinite
Knowing.

Somehow by this wonderful miracle called 'I Am' or
life, there is this infinite possibility of being the 'I' of
knowing the unseen (totally subjective) and the 'I' of
knowing form, made of 'What I Am', (still subjective,
no objects).

I am able to be omnipresent, able to know the deeper
opening of the unseen whilst also knowing my Self.
Now without objectifying a self on this level, but
knowing the Self as my Self . Do you see the
difference? No objects. Alignment happens.

I am no longer in fear, in distortion or pulled by the
leash of what I have made separate and more real than
'What I Am'. Now form is real, a level of Reality
having real form as pure aware Knowing.

In *The Form Reality Practice* this is this, the Infinity
Symbol: " I know I am and I know I am not. Formed
and formless. Omnipresence means to be the presence
and abide in the deep, whilst having living knowledge
and opening on both, the depths of the unseen and its
arising forms.

They are simply rising forms of what I-Awareness
realise in the unseen. Those forms rise immediately and
form. Immediately. They are not of space and time in
that they have no duration. They vibrate at the
frequency of Now.

This is actually what is making your body, the form on
this level, of the one who is listening to these words.
This is how Awareness, knowingly present and aware,
raises up the level of self; by not belonging to it, by not
listening to the conditionalities that are still vibing in
the fields of separation. Awareness is realising that
'What I Am' is beyond time and 'What I Am' is within
all times. I have never been anything else other than
'What Is'.

What You Are Searching for is Right Now

The Reality you are searching for is not distant, it is
right now. The goodness that you are seeking is right
now. It is the 'I' that is listening to these words now. It
has never gone anywhere. It is not in the future, it is not
in the past. This living essence, this living goodness is
now. It is nowhere else. It has been covered on this
level of form by objectifying Reality, objectifying a
sense of self and not clearly seeing that forms arise
within Awareness and Awareness moves those forms by
way of belonging to meaning or Knowing.

When Awareness (you and I) look at a form we
objectify that form as 'other'. We name or categorise it
in dualities of like or dislike. We do this mentally,
emotionally, psychologically, physically, psychically

and energetically. We are always splitting the atom, the
Atman or the presence of pure living Knowing-
Awareness into parts.

When you awaken, you are returning all those parts and
that power to the heart of Knowing. You will no longer
be seeing forms as objects. You will be knowing
directly as light streaming as pure living Awareness.

You are seeing Awareness and also knowing the split
you have created in body, mind and experience.
This will have a strong pull for you if you still favour
divided experience over deep Knowing or Truth, if you
value the experience registering in the body-mind over
direct and immediate Knowing, which is wholeness: 'I
Am that I Am', no separation.

In awakening your relationship will no longer be
objective, it will be subjective towards the 'I' that is
knowing 'I know'. That pulls the entire universe to
transform in your awareness and reform in this moment.

You are breathing the universe in, this universe called
'I'. It is changed within your deepening and re-formed. It
is all taking place Now. To really belong and value this
Knowing above any registration of experience in the
body-mind, is to return all the power that you have
separated into forms of separate experience to the
depths of realisation. Self-realisation; realising pure
Knowing now.

This is pure functionality on every level of Awareness
knowing it knows. There is never any object in it. There

is only the Self knowing itself in its own Self-radiant
experience: 'I am That'. Everything else is a division.

Awareness awakened to Itself brings every part of its
body, the legs of it, the arms of it, the eyes, the mouth,
the torso of it, back into pure subjectivity. The mother,
the father and the broken lover of it. Everything is
brought back within this moment of pure subjectivity.

This is not just self-mastery in that it is not mastery *over*
a self, it is the Master *within* the Self: Love. Love
makes it all good because Love is the one single Good
that has no opposite.

You decrease in the experience of being a 'someone' but
you increase in being the direct no-one, the no-body, a
power of Love, pure openness, of living Awareness that
pervades all. There is nothing it does not pervade and it
is the one who is listening to these words now. Return
your power of objectifying experience to direct heart
living Knowing, regardless of what registers in the
body-mind.

Abide in the deep, abide in the stillness. It Is not a blank
stillness, it Is not a 'duh…' stillness, it is *the* stillness. It
Is living, aware Knowing, sweet delight with endless
depths of mystery. A living essence of Pure Being that
opens up on the surface as Awareness returns the
surface of reality to the one that truly is, this 'I' that' is
listening to these words now.

The Ultimate Betrayal

What You Are is Awareness and it knows it is aware and that Knowing is the power of Love, which is streaming the entire reality. The one who is listening to these words now is a stream of that and yet the whole of that. It is streaming a level reality that seems like it is separate but it is actually the whole thing.

Begin to be aware that everything is arising in your awareness right now. Cease objectifying the listener, the speaker. You will be going against your own stream, because to form *What You Are* and know the form of *What You Are*, you are having to fall out of infinite Knowing. It is like a betrayal. This is why sometimes we feel ashamed to awaken. It is as if we betrayed 'I', the infinite God or Good but we have not. It betrays itself to realise what *it* is, because there is only this One. There is a bit of a joker within all of this.

I don't know if you have seen that. To have a finite form is to fall out of infinite Knowing, until one is ripe enough to be the infinite Knowing in a finite form. Give up objectifying and containing power for someone who doesn't exist. Only the Lord exists, or God, or the Self, 'I'.

Awaken to what you deeply are and are able to know and open to. Infinite ways of Pure Being, whilst having a seeming finite form that in one breath expands in the moment of truly forming what is infinite, as the ongoing evolution of this human level of reality. This knows no end.

Divining the Moment

Q: *I want to ask about shame and the origin of that.*

B: Shame moves along with blame, which moves along with anger. They all move together. They are a trio and they are moved by fear. Fear is what they are on.

Shame happens when Awareness identifies with the forms of experience and doesn't realise what it is, that what you are as a self and person is an illusion.

This is the tendency on this level of conditionality, which really is in the bright Reality-space of the one who truly is. Reality isn't the formed level. Reality is the light in which all experience and even the movement of the wholeness, the unseen, moves, lives and on this level, forms. On this level of reality then, which is form, infinite Knowing fell purposefully out of infinity for a finite moment of forming what infinity is.

When Awareness identifies only with what it has fallen into, which is the objective conditional experience of a self-centre, then you become the one that is doing all this in polarities of good and bad, right and wrong, up and down, in and out.

When Awareness identifies with the conditional level of reality, then we come upon this shame of 'I've got it wrong', or even the opposite polarity of 'I am right', all from a limited self-perspective, from the identification as Awareness with separate-sense experience.

When you are awakening, you turn your movement
away from trying to get everything right, which creates
a movement of getting everything wrong. This, coupled
with a deeper sense of Knowing, is the stirring of
energy that comes up in your body-mind as shame and
guilt. But really there is nothing you can do as a sense
of self. It is all being done. You are being drawn back
through self-experience and you are not to blame. To let
go of shame you have to pass through the whole game
and not look back.

Shame is the belief that you ever did anything. If you
are to realise the deep, you realise that nothing actually
ever happened. Yet the place that is streaming as
'nothing ever happened' is forming in a conditional
reality.

Shame simply comes through identification of separate-
sense experience, particularly when you begin to
awaken because you have a higher Knowing but you're
not applying the higher Knowing as Awareness
knowing it knows. You are applying it to a sense of self
that doesn't demonstrate this innocence, doesn't
demonstrate this movement, so guilt or blame or shame
arise.

Apply the higher Knowing and pass through any
experience of 'other', of shame or guilt or blame. Pass
through it without identification. Somehow this is a
growth movement, a movement of evolution. You pass
through conditional experiences that are well imprinted
into the present evolution of our societies, imprinted
like a groove.

You can pass through and know the groove but not
belong to it. You *will* pass through the experience of
those energies, which you are now not identifying with.

See that it is evolutionary movement and your heart will
begin to shine. You will return into the realisation that
you are freedom itself. You'll find there will be no
judgment of others who might convey a level of you
that is purveying shame or guilt or blame.

This is a relationship of the divine and the divine is the
one listening to these words now. Otherwise you are not
divining the moment but dividing it. When you finally
no longer divide the moment in otherness, in guilt,
blame or shame, you meet the end of fear.

The moment is divine and it is moved in a way of divine
revelation of Self to one's Self. That's how it is.
Thank you all for coming to this retreat. Thank you all
for fully partaking in 'not retreating'.

New Zealand Retreat

*"When you move the deep Knowing,
belonging to the miracle of experiencing
deep form as You,
the unthinkable begins to be known,
begins to manifest, not for you as a self,
but as what You have always been,
eternal Love."*

Opening Night

*"Nothing can replace the Beloved. Nothing.
No one. Anything whatsoever.
Nothing can replace the Beloved.
Love the Beloved, you will realise the Beloved.
Love the Beloved and you will realise
the Beloved is the only One that is here.
Then all your relationships
begin to move as the Beloved."*

One Magnificent Earth Heart

You have come to grace this earth with *What You Are*.
You have come to grace everyone that you have ever
known with *What You Are*. You have come this week to
meet what you believed you couldn't meet. You have
come completely by grace to move to the deeper level
that is calling and to make it real. Truly you can live
this for the rest of eternity.

In our being together, in our sharing together, we will
see that we are not thirty brains, we are one magnificent
earth brain, one magnificent earth heart, one universal
mind, one universal heart and we all have deep, deep
communion, already. We are not reading each other's
self because there is none, we are reading the
Beloved *as* the Beloved together.

Drop all the wonderful self-ideas that you need pain,
struggle and distress, that you must have it. You don't
actually need anything, because deeply you are already
whole. Just tenderly reach a little deeper, a little deeper,

a little deeper. In our conversations together reach a little deeper, a little deeper, a little deeper... You will begin to perceive so much more freshly, cleanly. Read the levels as Awareness, as Love. Read them!

All in an Instant

You are profound silence, light moving, streaming through the body-mind up from deeper levels. You are streaming up and then you are going into the sense of 'I', the sense of self and person and all the relatedness around that - all in an instant. This is how you can realise the universe is your greater body. Be open to deeply seeing what is actually taking place. Deeply see it!

The tendency of Awareness is to identify with the first familiar pattern. We choose it and the world teaches us to and yet we created the world - not the earth, the earth came out of what we are. We superimposed the pattern of the world onto the pristine earth that is here to make possible human forms of divinity.

You Are Called Way, Way Beyond

You realise that being here ruins how you expect your life to continue? It ruins your life from how you perceive through your sense of self. What I hope to bring about together is a deeper living way. We could be anywhere together, anywhere at all: in town, on the beach, in the living room or in this marquee and wherever you are, deeper streams of your love, deeper

streams of your being, greater depth of *What You Are* is
the one constant that is present.

We are not awakening to what most people believe they
are awakening to. Your mind is awakening to *You* who
is Awareness-Knowing, seeing *Now*, without
name, form or identity, who moves through all names,
all forms and all identities. That is truly what is present.

Awareness, the one who is listening to these words
now, tends to identify with the content of mind, which
means the content of life but in truth life has no
content. *Living* does. Living has lots of content but Life
has no content. What Life has is *What You Are*. Life is
streaming with *What You Are*.

We have all come together because we're called by the
same One we *are*. You could not be in this room or be
with an apparent other and talk so profoundly,
simply, tenderly or terribly about the Beloved and not
be called. We are together because we are called. Do
you recognise this?

Do you recognise you are called way beyond how you
relate to who you believe you are? Way beyond. Way
way beyond! Do you see and know you hear? You
know you hear. We are the Hearing knowing and the
Knowing hearing, the Seeing seeing. Recognise how
beautifully deeply you know without single use of self,
a single use of the brain, a single use of the world.
Nothing needed, no thought, no feeling needed. We
could say together: 'I know'.

Knowing, if who you are Awareness is available, takes you immediately into That that you know, which is That that you are. Nothing is needed to grasp this. That that is calling is the one you are with no self, no body, no mind, no brain, no thing. Very gently one begins to perceive finely, a fineness is known. Even the birdsong is pointing the way.

Notice how that fineness is streaming this moment of forming. Now Awareness is knowing beyond, knowing fineness, knowing forming and knowing all this moving up into form, which in truth is formless. No object in it, no objective. Still pure Knowing. Somehow you are noticing that the forming has the deep in it. The deep is already moving as forming and there is still no one there. You can come right to the surface. It is as if you have moved from deep dreamless sleep, moved from unimaginable depth up into a surface level of reality. Reality being the radiance of the deep, the one who is listening to these words now. Now there is a body made of the deep. It doesn't have a self as yet, it is sweet innocence like a baby, goldenness waiting to integrate up into the movement of form as you and I. Yet you and I, the one who is listening, including the speaker IS this.

We all sit together because the deep is calling to be realised; to realise That that I Am and to move knowingly, to perceive so deeply that the old mind falls away in the light of you belonging to the deep calling. You long so much to deeply realise *What You Are*. You also long to meet that with others. Even though in the deep you know there are no others, you long to stream it together, to be it together, to realise it increasingly deeper. You also know that it costs you everything you have ever believed in of a conditional nature. We know that it cost us to realise that the Beloved is speaking, the Beloved is seeing, the Beloved is hearing. The Beloved loves the Beloved and it is the one listening to these words.

When you move the deep Knowing, belonging to the miracle of experiencing the deep form as you, the unthinkable begins to be known, begins to manifest, not for you as a self, but *as* what you have always been, eternal Love. The invitation to realise the Source as one's real Self is everywhere. Most people's difficulty is the belief that the past can tell you who you are and the future is going to make you *What You Are*. That is not the truth. It is all wonderful revelation, revealing you to you, with everyone you meet. We begin to know, taste and realise that we are already Love.

Your Cup is Being Emptied

Your calling is deep and real. You love that much, you love the Beloved, the truth that much, that your cup is being emptied so that more of *What You Are* can be poured in. There are many ways to say this and they are all displayed in your life. All the resistance in your life is the persistence that you are a somebody, whereas truly you are a wonderful, wonderful nobody.

Day One

*"Awareness you are in your own self-creation of the
universe. Constantly. Truly a movement of Love.*

*Every challenge that seems to be in the outside
is your inside calling you
to recognise it and be one with it,
all the way up to the surface."*

Undo Your Obsession

Undo your obsession with believing you have a
beginning and an end. Undo it. Be the flow of
openness. Then all those levels that you meet from the
deeper heart opening actually call you to be deeply
deeply true. You make a connection with what you
are *first* in the deep. Now there is no challenge for you.
Those levels that might cause you disturbance, that are
distasteful to you are pointing to where they want to
come home to You, direct.

Let Your Openness Find its Wonderful Way

Humans have tension they have no idea they are giving
their attention or their energy to. When you open, which
is a state of Love, you will not find tension there. I
could pour water on the ground and it would find its
wonderful way. In the same way, let your openness find
its wonderful way.

Can you enjoy where you are? The mind says, where you are is in a garden, in this marquee, with these people. The mind or the self will give you the information that you are constantly referring 'You' with.

It gives you the information you refer to in terms of who, what and where you are. This is in fact the mind's purpose, to reflect to you *where* you are in *What You Are*. It will also work out what that is through where you have been, constantly recycling memory to know *where* you are in *What You Are*. The mind will tell you: "I am a man, a woman, a human, a this or that, an electrician, etc. ", which are all wonderful vehicles of a far greater movement and sourcing.

The question is, can we be in life and move without a pattern? It is rather like when we look at the weather forecast and it tells us: "The pattern for the next three days is this and then comes another pattern and then another." We do exactly the same in our lives, we have long range comfortable forecasts and when the forecast says that a particular pattern front is imminent we get the umbrella of self. But is any pattern permanent?

What is permanent amongst this moment? What is total, what is Source? What gives all this reality? Can we allow fear and not judge it? Can we allow self, limited or otherwise, and not judge it? Can we see without a pattern? Can we begin to see that patterns only move when Awareness participates within the pattern as its belief that the pattern is what It is?

In truth, there are endless levels of the radiance 'I Am' that I am in-streaming and moving and I occupy them all equally without any separation. I am one total movement. To me daily life here in this human form gives us an immense opportunity to realise 'What I Am'.

Please, keep your 'I' in your own heart as we share this Love together. It is not the speaker.

As you start to stabilise in the deeper levels of Knowing there is a brightness about it, a deeper realness. But once you come up into a sense of self you are going to be knowing yourself like you have never known yourself before. The belief was that you are a solid woman, a solid man made up of different parts of likes and dislikes. Patterns that you have added to you, patterns of your own making.

Where I am coming from, I am saying that you are not actually taking anything on from your parents' parents. I am saying you are 'the lot', right from the beginning. You *are* your parents' parents' parents. You *are* your ancestry. Don't you want to be that vast? There is nothing grandiose about it but there is a beautiful soft magnificence that is sublimely innocent and real. No one passed any patterns down to anyone. Awareness, you are in your own self-creation of the universe. Constantly. Truly, a movement of Love.

If one is to truly awaken, every challenge that seems to be in the outside is your inside calling you to recognise it and be one with it all the way up to the surface. Then there is transfiguration in the nervous system, in the body mind and a deeper level of the brain activates.

The brain is a magnificent instrument of Love. The deeper level of the brain can only open to the deeper level of your calling, otherwise it would be too much for your sense of self. There is an emergency cut off system, because that energy would be too much for how you have partitioned your self, where really you are the wholeness.

Your daily life is your moment to moment opportunity to realise *What You Are* more deeply and utterly and watch the miracle of your belonging to that come all the way up to the surface. In this, your life gets reconfigured by the deeper You.

You have to understand that the way that Awareness has put the human together cannot understand this. Your self cannot understand this, therefore it won't want anything to do with this. What is your self? Your self is you in forms of conditionality that you are holding together as if you are a someone. That is your self, small self we're talking about.
What it really is, is an amazing and constant opportunity to be the cup that the Real You, The Self pours into, direct. Your heart will be all different, your mind will be all different and be clear about this, your life will be all different.

If you are awakening but you want to keep your life the same, you are in for a bit of a struggle. Because in realising deeper your life will definitely change in terms of how you relate to *What You Are* and in terms of what comes towards you to show you how rooted you are in the deeper realisation of *What You Are*.

Every human opportunity is a reflection of what you are rooted in. The more you are rooted into the deeper levels of you, whilst still holding a relationship to your body-mind self as 'other'. You suffer and say you are confused, because as you realise deeper the pressure of the New, making known to You where your self is holding on, will be enormous. In fact it can cause mental, emotional and physical disease, human relatedness disease. We see this dis-ease on the planet.

When you belong to what you are awakening to, You who is aware of this moment *now*, and you relate to it with all that you are and all that you have, then all that you have now belongs to all that you are. That is how it transforms and you will be knowing every level of opportunity, every level that is missed, every level that is taken and claimed and every level of every level that is moving and transforming in what you are as Reality. In this way, everything that shows up in your life, everything without exception is allowed space in your sense of self, person, body, mind, heart and life totally.

What most of us do on the surface is that we engage life and each other as *living*. We engage it with all the patterns that have been here since the beginning of time. We are looking for freedom, which is our love but we are engaging with patterns that have nothing to do with what we are.

When you can stand in a pattern being true to the deep, the pattern shifts because you are no longer belonging to it. You are not making it a problem and it shifts and shapes the new reality into deeper forming of the light you are now realising as you.

This can wonderfully happen inside, between two people and even between a whole planetary consciousness...

What is really amazing and often not seen is that within moments of utter despair, right there is the possibility of an immense power of Love that opens your mind, your heart and your body to what you have been visiting in deep dreamless sleep and what you visit when you are true to the moment. A power that is ready for forming *as* You.

Day Two

*"Knowing isn't limited to knowing 'a thing';
it is simply knowing no-thing.
Knowing your Knowing doesn't need a content;
knowing 'I Am Knowing' is your infinite nature."*

You are Not a Polarised Entity

When you begin to awaken you realise how you have
individuated your bodily, emotional and mental
experience from the past. Because your body is a pure
receiver of what you believe is real. You are receiving
through the core of your brain, the pineal gland, which
one could say is your cosmic aerial. What you are as
Awareness is telling the brain the reality you want to
pick up and manifest.

The moment you choose, as if there is a good and bad,
right and wrong, up and down, your brain exists as a
polarised entity. Then you become that polarised entity
but you are not an entity, you are the power in and
beyond the universe. You are Love, golden - not you as
a person, a self. You in Being are 'good as gold' as they
say here in New Zealand, because you are the One
Good.

Move What You Awaken To

Deeper reality is not only present but is being realised,
not to be lived in some future point but to be *now*
moving. When you realise deeper reality, move what

you awaken to, belong to it. You will disappear into it and you will awaken *as* that reality in a living embodiment.

Total Embodiment

Pure Mind glows like a vast egg around the whole body. Some realisers have been painted as having realisation like a halo only around the head but it should be all encompassing. I am not saying those realisers, such as Jesus were limited, I am saying to whoever painted the halo: "Hey, lower! "

It is a total embodiment, not just 'up there'. The mind is fully illumined with the Source itself as the one who is listening to these words now, and the whole embodiment is a movement of the deep, coming out of the black.

Pure Awareness, moving, bursting into light *The* Self, and manifesting Reality in a multidimensional splendour, and it is here right now as apparent you and I.

You can directly experience the shift of Awareness, the shift of Consciousness. Deeper dimensions made real in your experience within and as the body - same One, not two.

Pure Poetry

To me life is pure poetry or pure music or pure Love
and all that moves is the creative imagination of the one
that is listening to these words now. Here, on this
seemingly surface level of the One, the One appears as
the many. The many are the One, make no mistake
about that, and the many can find the One as the one
that they are amongst the many. If you go deeper
though you are only the One and that is true aloneness.
It is your first form.

Day and Night

Even day is night. You just close your eyes and there it
is. To me, when we say: "Night, night" it means black.
Black, the return to nothing.

Instead of hello, you could say: "Light light", which
means the creative force is what you are in. "Night
night, light light!" - that is What Is and they move
together. You are nothing and everything in one breath.

No One And Nobody

In deep dreamless sleep you are no one and nobody,
beautifully so, and when you wake up in the morning
you first individualise what Nothing is.

Day Three

Being Weaned Off Past Identification

If you are awakening, you are being weaned off of the
need for manifest forms to tell you who you are.
Thought is a manifest form, feeling is a manifest form,
birdsong is, your body is, your spoken word is a
manifest form. So many manifest forms!

In awakening you are awakening to relate direct to your
being and to the Self. In truth there is no existence
without the light of the Self and its movement bringing
itself home to realise what it is. It is the one constant in
the universe.

This is why certain traditions beat a drum. It is the
rhythm in the universe, it is the rhythm in your heart. It
is the rhythm in your breath. You have taught your
mind, your brain to constantly register events and then

instantly individuate them as something that is happening to a someone. This then gets stored and it is called the subconscious.

In awakening, the subconscious opens up its forms but the deep also opens up its forms. There is a trade between your illusory forms, those that pass away, and your true form, the form of your being, which is greater reality, profoundly real and deep and does not pass away.

They trade places. This is what the movement of infinity ∞ truly is, until both circles are realised as one movement, the movement of the deep, the movement of a profound form, which is the light that manifests the cosmos. The body is a map or a microcosm of this and instantly, in the same moment that it manifests, it returns. That is the heartbeat.

When you awaken, you awaken to finer forms of your being, which are unseen forms, veiled forms of light or Being. This movement, which is not a process in *What You Are* but *is* a process at the level of self and person, is a calling to unveil your being to your awareness that is identified with illusory forms; immediate and direct.

Prior to awakening, the tendency in human beings is to read past form. We ascribe time to this but basically it is all past form. Time is past form. Present form or the form of your being is Now, it has no past or measurement.

When you awaken you are being weaned off of identification with all past form. Sometimes in the body you will be feeling terrible, mentally, emotionally you can feel awful, in fact devastated. You are undoing your attachment to illusory forms, forms that are passing away. You have to discover this, you who is aware, who is listening to these words now.

You begin to listen deeper in the beyond, in true form or realms of Being. You are discerning illusory forms of identification falling away whilst you are awakening to profounder levels of pure form, which is Being. You begin to live in the beyond.

Your old way of relating to form mentally, emotionally and physically begins to dwindle or fade. It appears to be difficult to be weaned off of this, difficult for a person, but Awareness is being weaned off of the person, the image and is being reacquainted, as Awareness with deeper realms of Being. Realms unseen but not unknowable.

Within this movement of being weaned off of form, our calling gets more profound and our willingness to deeply belong to that calling begins to build. In many ways awakening is a call to prayer.

Yes, but…

When we say: "Yes, but…", the 'Yes' is Self-knowledge and the 'but' is small-self-knowledge.

You have not yet perceived the speed by which you transcend the 'but' and enter the 'Yes' and move from the 'Yes' to the 'but'. It is so fast... it's now!

Now is The Opportunity to Fully Open

Right now, Awareness has the opportunity to fully open, fully open the body and the unseen levels of the body. Relaxation of Awareness opens deeper levels that are now available to you in the beyond and in your body.

With what you are in touch with now, you can discern what level of form you are on, you can discern the development of self and person from direct aware Knowing. Awareness can also discern, as you who knows it knows, not *things* but Knowing itself. You know you know.

Add anything to that and you begin to invest in forms once again, in terms of seen and known historical forms.

In many ways you are called to remain open, no matter what moves through that openness and discern deeply from the deeper levels of your being whilst old ways of knowing will surface on their way home through the 'I'.

Day Four

*"In truth there is no existence
without the light of the Self and its movement
bringing itself home to realise what it is.
It is the one constant in the universe."*

A Vast Space of Love

Anything in time or space cannot have any value for *What You Are* to move in. You cannot move in it. You won't be known. You won't be seen. You won't be knowing *What You Are*, direct.

Patterns are made in and of time. If you identify with a pattern you then are in and of time and you have a body of time. Running with that body of time within that pattern is a feeling-sense hijacked by time, an intelligence hijacked by time, experience hijacked by time. This is what a pattern is. You will only ever identify with patterns if you still believe you exist in time and not as pure knowing Awareness, who on this level has form.

Love does not exist in space, time, past or future. Love doesn't exist or move in any of that. You have been looking for Love in that, *as* that and this is why you cannot find it. It is not there, wrapped up in the belief that you can be Love tomorrow or wrapped in the belief that you were Love last week or thirty years ago when you had your first awakening.

If you had awakening thirty years ago and you knew
Love, you opened beyond space and time and you came
into what you already are, which is Love. Then we see
that what we have done with Love is that we have made
Love about space and time, about a particular person in
duality (I and someone else) and we have made Love
about an emotion linked to a thought, linked to events in
the past that I thought were Love. We are always held in
this idea of past in the hope that we get that love again
in the future wrapped around a space-time body that is
an utter illusion. And yet all this is appearing in a vast
space of Love - it is 'I' listening to these words now.
This is why when one has a deeper realisation one falls
into one's opening, one's *own* opening. You have
opened.

Life will conspire to open you, sometimes crack you
open, burn you open, push you open or you live as
openness in everything. Nonetheless, the opening is
what you *are* inside that opening. The shell is the
appearance of forms of that opening. We relate to Love
as 'other', as a feeling as a sensation, and we continue
that relationship through past events that we thought
gave us Love. What actually happened is that we
opened beyond our limited sense of self and person and
Love streamed through and up into the levels of
form, such as the sense of self and person.

Because we have identified with space in time and our
bodies being in space and time, we have identified with
Love in a particular manner of polarity. We need
particular similar events and everything needs to be
'right' for Love to happen. But Love is all that is taking
place!

We can see how we patterned Love to need a particular form, along with a particular thought, a particular sensation that matches where we think we knew Love. We keep patterning this but Love is the opening in which the outpouring Love forms the universe and it is 'I' listening to these words now. So is Love something that you can speak about in the past or is Love the outpouring of openness?

When you identify with the body-mind in the morning, instantly you close down the openness and you then are moving as the pattern. You might think it is your pattern but it is humanity's pattern on this level of reality until it is gone.

Gone either by immersion into what the openness is as One Self or by events because we lack the true movement of Love in our meditation and enjoyment of life. When we believe: 'someone is the cause of my pain' it is not openness flowing, is not a true meditation of forms. You are opening forms in the belief that they are from the past but they are forms pouring out into reality here and now and have no past.

It starts with you looking into the bathroom mirror and believing that is 'you'. It starts with a thought you identify 'you' with, that immediately attaches to your name. A baby would confirm: "I am no body." Become as a child and discover that.

Much of our suffering and our difficulty is our inability to be the openness that we already are and fall deeper into that openness without reserve. We teach ourselves to reserve ourselves on so many levels. We hang onto the belief that we need something to be this Love and we do not. We simply need to fall into the deep, the abyss, the 'prior to' becoming anything. Then forms are the living forms of that newness.

If we don't go into this in our lives, then this is just a show, just mere entertainment. Sometimes, quite often actually, when one realises deeper, it is a bit of a quake where all your old forms fall into. But that is how you discover you stand free of your forms. You just think that they are you. Life gives you the opportunity to know the deep deeply and then it forms. Then you really know You are in the deep, a divine Creator, pouring out of the spaciousness and manifesting what you are in in the deep.

When We Speak Truth Together

You are looking at 'him' (B) and he is looking at you but that is a stream of light where the Self knows itself. It looks like you are looking at him and it looks like he is looking at you but truly it is God knowing God. Add images forms and sensations to that and it separates and individuates. If you don't do that, everyone in this room will realise Oneness - really *in* the body. When we deeply speak Truth together – not 'my truth', but Truth, it unites the field in the One that truly is.

Profound Caregivers for Love to Know Itself

I am using the analogy of a parent in terms of a profound caregiver for Love to know itself in the body; fully embodied. A parent is a profound caregiver. If parents loved the child utterly as the appearance of spaciousness coming up to form, selflessly and utterly, would the world be different? Or do we just continue passing on a shape of Love as a pattern but not as the true nature of Consciousness?

Would the world be different if parents would remain in the open womb that the child was conceived in, where beings merged and invited other beings into embodiment, so they could meet in the flesh and in Being and therefore manifest the universe in a profounder deepening moving reality - the movement of Love? If it were truly like that, would much of what we experience on the planet take place as it does?

Day Five

*"Freedom is not freedom from something.
Freedom is freedom AS everything."*

A Hall of Mirrors

When you are awakening it is as if you enter a hall of
mirrors in your self and in your person. It is a hall of
mirrors but the light is the same un-refracted light. It is
all a reflection leading back to the same One who is
knowing. All this is a hall of mirrors but you are called
to the great Hall where true radiance is. This is where
you want to abide as Awareness. That is true aware
Knowing.

It looks like 'someone' is awakening but in truth the
Only One is eternally awakening. Eternally, without
beginning and end, awakening in the liquid forms of
light that settle in form. Life comes from a liquid form
of light, like a volcano. The lava now seems to be static,
growing life forms but it is not. If you go into what was
once lava, you will see it is still moving. Now it is
moving as life forms, all endeavouring to remember the
fire they came out of. It is really like this. The earth is
such a wonderful mirror of what is deeply, deeply real,
veiled only by the illusion of 'other'.

As Awareness directly awakening, this will have your
body, your self and your person immediately. You will
be knowing the divine work or the deep work of the
deep unveiling itself, no matter who it seems to be. The
unveiling of the same One to the same One, no matter

who it seems to be and no matter how that first, let's call it explosion of the interior, landed, moved, formed and is now growing and evolving. It is still the same One. When it lands here it individuates a little. It looks like a lot but it is just a little, maybe three percent, but what is three percent of a powerful output of Source? That is a great deal moving. Every apparent individual has immense power as a being and that power is literally manifesting the life.

When Awareness gives its power to the illusion of separation, it builds a separate sense of self only to return that seemingly separate sense of self, which begins in waking up to mirror the intensity of the undoing, the intensity of the unveiling of the power given away to separateness, to individuate what *it* is. It is doing it to itself! No one is doing it.

'I Am' the One that is moving this, the one who is listening to these words now, appearing to be someone amongst the crowd, but 'I Am' amongst my own radiant self-forms in the volcanic eruption of my calling to express 'What I Am' into all manner of forms, all manner of levels of intelligence, all manner of vibrant beings that are all masked until called. Called in terms of the highest, highest possibility.

The calling is always *now*. People relate that to having distance. Self-realisation is: 'there is no distance', there is no space and time that divides the One from its true forms. That is awakening. To truly engage that in life is to immediately affect untold change, which appears to be devastating to the old sense of self you once moved with.

You cannot mix the old way with the first way of light moving. You cannot mix it. You think you can mix it because you are this artful being that is able to instantly be and believe you are a whole-body, wholly *What You Are*, but you are a mix of levels. You can have deeper realisation and still keep your old ways and move a little of the new way. That is confusion and pain and suffering on the outside.

Everything is a hall of mirrors reflecting the Oneness to the One and also reflecting all the disjointedness. It is the Self, the Supreme Self, as Awareness avoiding all the mirrors. IT is the light, reflected or not - unchanged Knowing, unaltered by the many mirrors. Only seemingly so.

The light of Knowing is only knowing its own light, aware and real. Refracted light means you look in the past and have a future and it is definitely a hall of mirrors and not one glow, one whole bright reality. When Awareness drops a little into the truth of what truly is and doesn't divide that into 'other' then what seems to be difficult and painful is simply the shedding of the old way and the movement of the new that has no need of past, that is now moving.

Awareness begins to see that what it is at source is already flourishing, no matter what takes place in the hall of mirrors. It all comes from and returns to the 'great hall', where nothing ever happens. There will always be a hall of mirrors and a great hall, to which the refracted light returns to know itself. It returns each refraction to the great hall, which means the whole. That is the cosmic game and the one who is listening is even beyond all that. So, paying attention to what is moving is foolish. Giving your power to what is truly moving it, is wisdom.

That is the impulse that is moving the whole of life throughout the cosmos. You are realising 'home' deeper, whilst that gets expressed as new life and an entirely new way. The relating you have to the body-mind, thought and feeling is changed. You are now seeing from a deeper place, which gives you true perspective in what is taking place in mind, in will, in body, in life. You now have one relationship only, to the depth and it is not divided, no matter what happens in the hall of mirrors.

You begin to love it. You begin to love how that one is awakening and unveiling in and as You. This is the Real You unveiling itself to itself. Creation is IT veiled, unveiling IT.

This can come down right down to this very place – right here. But 'here' the hall of mirrors is going to go "Whooooooosh" and "Whoooooom!" If you are not ready for that sound, it will be far too much for you. It is actually the sound of you coming out and going in, coming out whilst going up coming down, going out, coming in. It is one unbelievable movement of True You.

You love it. But to love it and to discover that love you will need to be loving others as your own self. You won't find it any other way. This ends on this level, the light needing to split itself into mirrors. You realise that

everything is already shining and there is no refraction;
a flower is as much the Godhead as one who realises
in human form.

Called Beyond Distraction

Awakening Awareness is called to go beyond all
distraction, all contraction, all inflammation and be its
first light and movement. This will change the world we
apparently live in.

You are never up *against* society or up *against* your
family. You who is aware in the light of Awareness are
always meeting what is out-flowed and becomes solid
identification.

I have been here since the beginning of time and I Am
here at the end and I discover I Am not a beginning or
an end. If you enter society as what you are *first*, you
transform it, because you are what made it.

You are prior to all relatedness. Relate only to that
Knowing in all your relationships, that is how the
universe is born.

Then you are not growing in strength you are revealing
simplicity which has untold mystery and power that
never gets used by anybody.

About B

"When I say 'I', I am not speaking of someone called B
Prior I am speaking as the only 'I' in the universe that is
emptiness and yet full."

B offers a profoundly unique and enlightening
perspective on life from the smallest matters that shape
our personal lives to the biggest universal questions of
human existence. His teaching and transmission is the
ultimate calling to awaken as Awareness-Knowing.

With true compassion, humour and uncompromising
Truth, B brings the highest teaching straight to our core
and into daily life. His call is to profoundly awaken
whilst living in the world and his discourses cover all
areas of life - relationships, sexuality, work and
creativity, parenting and children, all brought to an
awakening heart of Conscious Awareness.

Born in 1954 in England, B's childhood and teenage
years were marked by profound mystical experiences.
At age 19 he awakened in the realisation of Oneness
and at 33 he opened into the Absolute. Within this
unfolding he was graced with the rare and profound
realisation of the Bhagavati, the divine Feminine
Principle. Following realisation his known life up to
that point was entirely shattered. A life of service in
utter dedication to the awakening and evolution of
humanity began and continues to unfold.

B is the Originator of *The Form Reality Practice*, a
powerful movement practice and vehicle of awakening
that is the living embodiment and transmission of
realisation.

He currently lives in New Zealand and travels
extensively offering talks, seminars and residential
retreats.

"A Master is a location of infinite Consciousness that is no-thing yet it is locatable. You dive into that Master and you are no longer going to be locatable."

Those Who Come

My knowledge is that those that come - to 'him' (B) have prepared the ground of their life to be more than the conditional sense of self. Otherwise you could not be here with this one. It would be too much for how you have put your sense of self together. By the way, it will feel like that at times. I suggest that this is what you come into: to flow more of the deeper realisation and to make real in your body what you are realising.

You have to understand that your life of how you have lived it so far is at an end. Only then are there new beginnings. All that you will ever meet is the shadow of old form, whilst you are directly meeting the light forming. You are individualising in this moment, your ability to be the same One as you address another and unite with each and every soul in wholeness for they are the same One, evolving every level of the universe without beginning or end.

This is the pouring of Love. Infinity in a moment of quantum finiteness called 'I' and how that moment of quantum finiteness can meet another exactly in the same place and realise Oneness is total already.

I am suggesting that the human brain will eventually melt together and become one, because what you are is rebirthing this moment as you truly awaken and you let go of the fear in the belief that you are limited. You do not have a beginning or end. You are already radiant freedom. All this is just one wonderful level of YOU.

Also by B Prior

Love Without Duality - Awakening in Intimacy

Love Knowing, Moving, Manifesting the Deep

To find out more about B Prior's
teaching and events worldwide, go to:

www.bprior.org

or contact:

B Prior Foundation
30 Teddington Rd
Governors Bay 8971

info@bernieprior.org
+64 3 3299 135